PRACTICE - ASSESS - DIAGNOSE

180 Days of WRITING for Sixth Grade

- Prewriting
- Drafting
- Revising
- Editing
- Publishing

Author
Wendy Conklin, M.A.

SHELL EDUCATION

Standards

For information on how this resource meets national and other state standards, see pages 4–6. You may also review this information by scanning the QR code or visiting our website at http://www.shelleducation.com and following the on-screen directions.

Publishing Credits

Corinne Burton, M.A.Ed., *President*; Emily R. Smith, M.A.Ed., *Content Director*; Jennifer Wilson, *Editor*; Grace Alba Le, *Multimedia Designer*; Don Tran, *Production Artist*; Stephanie Bernard, *Assistant Editor*; Amber Goff, *Editorial Assistant*

Image Credits

pp. 61, 71, 79, 117–118, 95, 135–138, 151, 193: iStock; All other images Shutterstock

Standards

© Copyright 2010. National Governors Association Center for Best Practices and Council of Chief State School Officers. All rights reserved. (CCSS)

Shell Education

5301 Oceanus Drive
Huntington Beach, CA 92649-1030
http://www.shelleducation.com
ISBN 978-1-4258-1529-5
© 2015 Shell Education Publishing, Inc.

TABLE OF CONTENTS

INTRODUCTION

The Need for Practice

To be successful in today's writing classrooms, students must deeply understand both concepts and procedures so that they can discuss and demonstrate their understanding. Demonstrating understanding is a process that must be continually practiced for students to be successful. Practice is especially important to help students apply their concrete, conceptual understanding of each particular writing skill.

Understanding Assessment

In addition to providing opportunities for frequent practice, teachers must be able to assess students' writing skills. This is important so that teachers can adequately address students' misconceptions, build on their current understandings, and challenge them appropriately. Assessment is a long-term process that involves careful analysis of student responses from a discussion, project, practice sheet, or test. When analyzing the data, it is important for teachers to reflect on how their teaching practices may have influenced students' responses and to identify those areas where additional instruction may be required. In short, the data gathered from assessments should be used to inform instruction: slow down, speed up, or reteach. This type of assessment is called *formative assessment*.

HOW TO USE THIS BOOK

With *180 Days of Writing*, creative, theme-based units guide students as they practice the five steps of the writing process: prewriting, drafting, revising, editing, and publishing. During each odd week (Weeks 1, 3, 5, etc.), students interact with mentor texts. Then, students apply their learning by writing their own pieces during each following even week (Weeks 2, 4, 6, etc.). Many practice pages also focus on grammar/language standards to help improve students' writing.

Easy to Use and Standards Based

These daily activities reinforce grade-level skills across the various genres of writing: argument, informative/explanatory, and narrative. Each day provides a full practice page, making the activities easy to prepare and implement as part of a classroom morning routine, at the beginning of each writing lesson, or as homework.

The chart below indicates the writing and language standards that are addressed throughout this book. See pages 5–6 for a breakdown of which writing standard is covered in each week. **Note:** Students may not have deep understandings of some topics in this book. Remember to assess students based on their writing skills and not their content knowledge.

College and Career Readiness Standards

Writing 6.1—Write arguments to support claims with clear reasons and relevant evidence.
Writing 6.2—Write informative/explanatory texts to examine a topic and convey ideas, concepts, and information through the selection, organization, and analysis of relevant content.
Writing 6.3—Write narratives to develop real or imagined experiences or events using effective technique, relevant descriptive details, and well-structured event sequences.
Language 6.1—Demonstrate command of the conventions of standard English grammar and usage when writing or speaking.
Language 6.2—Demonstrate command of the conventions of standard English capitalization, punctuation, and spelling when writing.
Language 6.3—Use knowledge of language and its conventions when writing, speaking, reading, or listening.
Language 6.5—Demonstrate understanding of figurative language, word relationships, and nuances in word meanings.

HOW TO USE THIS BOOK (cont.)

Below is a list of overarching themes, corresponding weekly themes, and the writing standards that students will encounter throughout this book. For each overarching theme, students will interact with mentor texts in the odd week and then apply their learning by writing their own pieces in the even week. **Note:** The writing prompt for each week can be found on pages 7–8. You may wish to display the prompts in the classroom for students to reference throughout the appropriate weeks.

Overarching Themes	Weekly Themes	Standards
Adventures	**Week 1:** Places I've Been **Week 2:** Places I Want to Go	**Writing 6.3**—Write narratives to develop real or imagined experiences or events using effective technique, relevant descriptive details, and well-structured event sequences.
Greek Mythology	**Week 3:** Gods and Heroes **Week 4:** Nature of the World	**Writing 6.2**—Write informative/explanatory texts to examine a topic and convey ideas, concepts, and information through the selection, organization, and analysis of relevant content.
Fairy Tales	**Week 5:** Fairy Tales: For Children or Adults? **Week 6:** Fairy Tales: A Villain's Perspective	**Writing 6.1**—Write arguments to support claims with clear reasons and relevant evidence.
Mysteries	**Week 7:** Unsolved Mysteries **Week 8:** Ghosts	**Writing 6.1**—Write arguments to support claims with clear reasons and relevant evidence.
Medieval Times	**Week 9:** Living as Royalty **Week 10:** Living as Peasants	**Writing 6.3**—Write narratives to develop real or imagined experiences or events using effective technique, relevant descriptive details, and well-structured event sequences.
Renaissance	**Week 11:** Renaissance Artists **Week 12:** Renaissance Inventions	**Writing 6.3**—Write narratives to develop real or imagined experiences or events using effective technique, relevant descriptive details, and well-structured event sequences.
Explorers	**Week 13:** Pirates and Treasures **Week 14:** Adventures into the Unknown	**Writing 6.3**—Write narratives to develop real or imagined experiences or events using effective technique, relevant descriptive details, and well-structured event sequences.
Engineering	**Week 15:** Building Bridges **Week 16:** Designing Parachutes	**Writing 6.2**—Write informative/explanatory texts to examine a topic and convey ideas, concepts, and information through the selection, organization, and analysis of relevant content.
Calendar Events	**Week 17:** Groundhog Day **Week 18:** Daylight Saving Time	**Writing 6.1**—Write arguments to support claims with clear reasons and relevant evidence.

HOW TO USE THIS BOOK (cont.)

Overarching Themes	Weekly Themes	Standards
Superheroes	**Week 19:** Superhero Origins **Week 20:** Superhero Powers	**Writing 6.2**—Write informative/explanatory texts to examine a topic and convey ideas, concepts, and information through the selection, organization, and analysis of relevant content.
Outer Space	**Week 21:** Black Holes **Week 22:** Space Travel	**Writing 6.2**—Write informative/explanatory texts to examine a topic and convey ideas, concepts, and information through the selection, organization, and analysis of relevant content.
Scripts	**Week 23:** Live Theater Scripts **Week 24:** Television Show Scripts	**Writing 6.3**—Write narratives to develop real or imagined experiences or events using effective technique, relevant descriptive details, and well-structured event sequences.
Newspaper	**Week 25:** Cartoon Strips **Week 26:** Movie Reviews	**Writing 6.1**—Write arguments to support claims with clear reasons and relevant evidence.
Fantasy	**Week 27:** Fantasy Creatures **Week 28:** Fantasy Quests	**Writing 6.3**—Write narratives to develop real or imagined experiences or events using effective technique, relevant descriptive details, and well-structured event sequences.
Fairness	**Week 29:** Rights and Equality **Week 30:** Diversity	**Writing 6.1**—Write arguments to support claims with clear reasons and relevant evidence.
Interesting Sports	**Week 31:** Lacrosse **Week 32:** Rugby	**Writing 6.2**—Write informative/explanatory texts to examine a topic and convey ideas, concepts, and information through the selection, organization, and analysis of relevant content.
Pets	**Week 33:** Domestic Pets **Week 34:** Exotic Pets	**Writing 6.2**—Write informative/explanatory texts to examine a topic and convey ideas, concepts, and information through the selection, organization, and analysis of relevant content.
Health	**Week 35:** Eating **Week 36:** Exercising	**Writing 6.1**—Write arguments to support claims with clear reasons and relevant evidence.

HOW TO USE THIS BOOK (cont.)

Weekly Setup

Write each prompt on the board throughout the appropriate week. Students should reference the prompts as they work through the activity pages so that they stay focused on the topics and the right genre of writing: argument, informative/explanatory, and narrative. You may wish to print copies of this chart from the Digital Resource CD (filename: writingprompts.pdf) and distribute them to students to keep throughout the school year.

Week	Prompt
1	Imagine that you are taking a trip that goes terribly wrong. Describe the experience, including where you went and what went wrong.
2	Imagine that you have just taken a trip of a lifetime. Describe the experience, including where you went and what you did.
3	Greeks used mythology for several reasons. Explain some of the reasons and why the reasons are important.
4	Create your own myth about a natural phenomenon. Include details about what makes the phenomenon happen.
5	Do you think fairy tales are more for children or for adults? Include reasons to support your argument.
6	Do you think fairy tales would or would not be better if they were told from the villains' perspectives? Include reasons to support your argument.
7	Who do you think is responsible for the crime, Chet or Ginger? Include reasons to support your claim.
8	Do you think a ghost delivered the cupcake in the story on page 49? Use details to support your argument.

Week	Prompt
9	Imagine you are witnessing a peasant approach a lord during the medieval time period. Describe the events of what happens.
10	Imagine you are a peasant living during the medieval time period. Describe one day, including whom you speak with and the events that take place.
11	Think about a Renaissance artist. Write a narrative about the artist and his or her work. Include details about how the artist felt at the time.
12	Imagine you are living during the Renaissance. Write about a Renaissance invention, and describe how it can change the way people live or learn.
13	Imagine you are a pirate on an adventure. Write a narrative that describes your adventure and what you discovered.
14	Imagine you are an explorer. Write a narrative that describes your adventure and what you discovered.
15	Explain the differences between beam, suspension, truss, and arch bridges.
16	Explain the differences between round, ribbon-ring, ram-air, and square parachutes.

HOW TO USE THIS BOOK *(cont.)*

Week	Prompt
17	Do you think Groundhog Day should be celebrated? Provide details to support your argument.
18	Do you think daylight saving time is necessary? Provide details to support your argument.
19	Choose a superhero. Describe the superhero and include facts about how the superhero came to be.
20	Explain how super powers are beneficial to superheroes and everyday citizens.
21	Describe what black holes are. Include details about their sizes and where they are located.
22	Explain some of the preparations NASA is making for future space travel.
23	Write a theater script. Be sure to focus on one event and include multiple characters.
24	Write a script for a scene in a new television show. Be sure to focus on one event and include multiple characters.
25	Create a comic strip. Be sure to include at least two characters, a problem, a solution, and a moral.
26	Think about a movie you have seen. Write a review for it. Be sure to state your opinion of the movie and provide evidence to support your opinion.
27	Write a narrative about at least one fantasy creature. Describe the events that happen to the fantasy creature(s).
28	Imagine that you are a wizard about to embark on a daring adventure. Describe the events of your journey, including what happens and whom you meet along the way.

Week	Prompt
29	Do you think equal rights are still being talked about today? Write your argument and include details to support your argument.
30	Do you think diversity is important in a classroom? Write your argument and include details to support your argument.
31	Explain how the game of lacrosse is played. Include details to make it easy to understand.
32	Explain how the game of rugby is played. Include details to make it easy to understand.
33	There are many reasons people have domestic pets. Write a paragraph explaining what owning a pet entails.
34	Choose an exotic pet. Then, write a paragraph explaining the characteristics of that animal.
35	Some people think eating healthy is a must, while others think it is not something to worry about. Explain which side you support and why.
36	Some people think exercising is a good thing, while others think it is not a good thing. Explain which side you support and why.

#51529—180 Days of Writing

HOW TO USE THIS BOOK (cont.)

Using the Practice Pages

The activity pages provide practice and assessment opportunities for each day of the school year. Teachers may wish to prepare packets of weekly practice pages for the classroom or for homework. As outlined on pages 5–6, each two-week unit is aligned to one writing standard. **Note:** Before implementing each week's activity pages, review the corresponding prompt on pages 7–8 with students and have students brainstorm thoughts about each topic.

On odd weeks, students practice the daily skills using mentor texts. On even weeks, students use what they have learned in the previous week and apply it to their own writing.

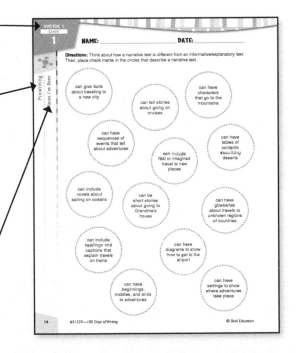

Each day focuses on one of the steps in the writing process: prewriting, drafting, revising, editing, and publishing.

There are 18 overarching themes. Each odd week and the following even week focus on unique themes that fit under one overarching theme. For a list of the overarching themes and individual weekly themes, see pages 5–6.

Using the Resources

The following resources will be helpful to students as they complete the activity pages. Print copies of these resources and provide them to students to keep at their desks.

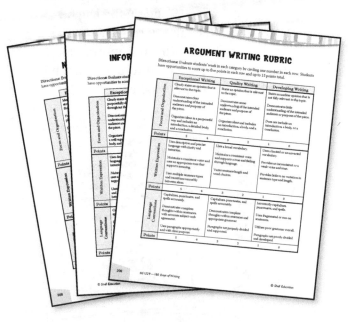

Rubrics for the three genres of writing (argument, informative/explanatory, and narrative) can be found on pages 206–208. Use the rubrics to assess students' writing at the end of each even week. Be sure to share these rubrics with students often so that they know what is expected of them.

HOW TO USE THIS BOOK *(cont.)*

Using the Resources *(cont.)*

The Writing Process can be found on page 212 and on the Digital Resource CD (filename: writingprocess.pdf). Students can reference each step of the writing process as they move through each week.

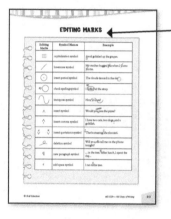

Editing Marks can be found on page 213 and on the Digital Resource CD (filename: editingmarks.pdf). Students may need to reference this page as they work on the editing activities (Day 4s).

If you wish to have students peer or self-edit their writing, a *Peer/Self-Editing Checklist* is provided on page 220 and on the Digital Resource CD (filename: editingchecklist.pdf).

Writing Signs for each of the writing genres are on pages 217–219 and on the Digital Resource CD (filename: writingsigns.pdf). Hang the signs up during the appropriate two-week units to remind students which type of writing they are focusing on.

Writing Tips pages for each of the writing genres can be found on pages 214–216 and on the Digital Resource CD (filename: writingtips.pdf). Students can reference the appropriate *Writing Tips* pages as they work through the weeks.

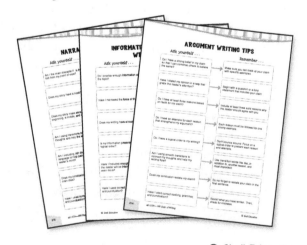

HOW TO USE THIS BOOK *(cont.)*

Diagnostic Assessment

Teachers can use the practice pages as diagnostic assessments. The data analysis tools included with the book enable teachers or parents to quickly score students' work and monitor their progress. Teachers and parents can quickly see which writing skills students may need to target further to develop proficiency.

After students complete each two-week unit, score each students' even week Day 5 published piece using the appropriate, genre-specific rubric (pages 206–208). Then, complete the *Practice Page Item Analysis* (pages 209–211) that matches the writing genre. These charts are also provided on the Digital Resource CD as PDFs, Microsoft Word® files, and Microsoft Excel® files (filenames: argumentpageitem.pdf, argumentpageitem.doc, argumentpageitem.xls; informativepageitem.pdf, informativepageitem.doc, informativepageitem.xls; narrativepageitem.pdf, narrativepageitem.doc, narrativepageitem.xls). Teachers can input data into the electronic files directly on the computer, or they can print the pages and analyze students' work using paper and pencil.

To Complete the Practice Page Item Analyses:

- Write or type students' names in the far-left column. Depending on the number of students, more than one copy of the form may be needed or you may need to add rows.

- The weeks in which the particular writing genres are the focus are indicated across the tops of the charts. **Note:** Students are only assessed on the even weeks, therefore the odd weeks are not included on the charts.

- For each student, record his or her rubric score in the appropriate column.

- Add the scores for each student after they've focused on a particular writing genre twice. Place that sum in the far right column. Use these scores as benchmarks to determine how each student is performing. This allows for three benchmarks during the year that you can use to gather formative diagnostic data.

HOW TO USE THIS BOOK *(cont.)*

Using the Results to Differentiate Instruction

Once results are gathered and analyzed, teachers can use the results to inform the way they differentiate instruction. The data can help determine which writing types are the most difficult for students and which students need additional instructional support and continued practice.

Whole-Class Support

The results of the diagnostic analysis may show that the entire class is struggling with a particular writing genre. If these concepts have been taught in the past, this indicates that further instruction or reteaching is necessary. If these concepts have not been taught in the past, this data is a great preassessment and may demonstrate that students do not have a working knowledge of the concepts. Thus, careful planning for the length of the unit(s) or lesson(s) must be considered, and additional front-loading may be required.

Small-Group or Individual Support

The results of the diagnostic analysis may show that an individual student or a small group of students is struggling with a particular writing genre. If these concepts have been taught in the past, this indicates that further instruction or reteaching is necessary. Consider pulling these students aside to instruct them further on the concept(s), while others are working independently. Students may also benefit from extra practice using games or computer-based resources. Teachers can also use the results to help identify individual students or groups of proficient students who are ready for enrichment or above-grade-level instruction. These students may benefit from independent learning contracts or more challenging activities.

Digital Resource CD

The Digital Resource CD contains digital copies of the activity pages, the diagnostic pages, and additional resources, such as the *Editing Marks* and *Writing Tips* pages, for the students. The list of resources on the Digital Resource CD can be found on page 221.

STANDARDS CORRELATIONS

Shell Education is committed to producing educational materials that are research and standards based. In this effort, we have correlated all of our products to the academic standards of all 50 states, the District of Columbia, the Department of Defense Dependents Schools, and all Canadian provinces.

How to Find Standards Correlations

To print a customized correlation report of this product for your state, visit our website at http://www.shelleducation.com and follow the on-screen directions. If you require assistance in printing correlation reports, please contact our Customer Service Department at 1-877-777-3450.

Purpose and Intent of Standards

Legislation mandates that all states adopt academic standards that identify the skills students will learn in kindergarten through grade twelve. Many states also have standards for Pre-K. This same legislation sets requirements to ensure the standards are detailed and comprehensive.

Standards are designed to focus instruction and guide adoption of curricula. Standards are statements that describe the criteria necessary for students to meet specific academic goals. They define the knowledge, skills, and content students should acquire at each level. Standards are also used to develop standardized tests to evaluate students' academic progress.

Teachers are required to demonstrate how their lessons meet state standards. State standards are used in the development of all of our products, so educators can be assured they meet the academic requirements of each state.

The activities in this book are aligned to today's national and state-specific college and career readiness standards. The chart on page 4 lists the writing and language standards used throughout this book. A more detailed chart on page 5–6 correlates the specific writing standards to each week. The standards charts are also on the Digital Resource CD (filename: standards.pdf).

NAME: _____ DATE: _____

Prewriting
Places I've Been

Directions: Think about how a narrative text is different from an informative/explanatory text. Then, place check marks in the circles that describe a narrative text.

can give facts about traveling to a new city

can tell stories about going on cruises ✓

can have characters that go to the mountains ✓

can have sequences of events that tell about adventures ✓

can include real or imagined travel to new places ✓

can have tables of contents describing deserts

can include novels about sailing on oceans ✓

can be short stories about going to Grandma's house ✓

can have glossaries about travels to unknown regions of countries

can include headings and captions that explain travels on trains

can have diagrams to show how to get to the airport

can have beginnings, middles, and ends to adventures ✓

can have settings to show where adventures take place ✓

#51529—180 Days of Writing

NAME: _____ **DATE:** _____

Directions: Read the paragraph. Find at least three places where more details are needed to make the story more exciting. Underline these areas, and make notes in the margins about what you might add to the story.

Nothing exciting ever happens when we travel to Grandma's house. We always stop for food and gas at the same places. We never have to ask how much longer because we know all the markers on the ~~highway. We see the same sights on our journeys . . . until last year.~~ *explain how you* That was the year that they closed the highway, and we had to find another route. The first place we stopped at was the gas station. The restroom was not even in working order! That was bad news because all the snacks in our car were ruined when my little brother spilled his milk. Then, when we tried to find a suitable place to eat dinner, we ended up eating bland fast food. Then, the worst thing happened, but I won't talk about it now. Somehow, we made it to Grandma's, relieved to have lived through that adventure and hoping to never repeat it again!

explain why closed

explain why you're so harsh on the places you go to eat.

Cursive Practice *abc*

Directions: Use cursive to write at least two sentences that tell how you would feel if you experienced the adventure above.

The ride was boring.
But, it was fun to see
Grandma

Revising

Places I've Been

NAME: _____ DATE: _____

Directions: Read the sentences. Use numbers to reorder the sentences so that the story makes sense. Then, answer the questions.

_3_ But then, her lungs grew accustomed to the altitude.

_5_ Only then did it dawn on her that she might not be able to find her way back to the village.

_1_ When she pulled on the cord, the balloon began to rise far into the sky.

_4_ Farther and farther she flew until she couldn't see her village anymore.

_2_ At first, the thin air took her breath away.

1. Why is order important to the story?

Because it wouldn't make sense if the order was different

2. What feelings do you think the character might be experiencing throughout the story?

scared, adventerous, nervous

NAME: _____ DATE:_____

Directions: Use the ✒ symbol to replace the underlined pronouns in the sentences below and make them correct.

1. If a student really wants to have fun, <u>they</u> can go to the backyard for an afternoon adventure.

2. Most students enjoy flying on planes instead of driving to the mountains because it takes too long for <u>he or she</u> to reach their final destinations.

3. Whenever one spends time in the rainforest, <u>you</u> has to be ready for the rain showers at any moment.

4. The train zoomed past <u>she and him</u> so fast that their tickets blew from their hands.

5. When Emily went to the secret garden, <u>they</u> had to be careful of the poisonous flowers.

Boost Your Learning! 🚀

Inappropriate pronoun shifts happen when a sentence shifts between first person (*I, we*), to second person (*you*), or third person (*he, she, they*). Be sure to stay with the original pronouns when writing narratives.

Example: We loved going to the zoo last summer. We learned

that ∧^{we}you could hold the snakes in the reptile room!

NAME: _____ DATE:_____

Directions: Read the paragraph. Use what you have learned this week to make the story more exciting. Revise the story by adding details on the lines provided.

Nothing exciting ever happens when we travel to Grandma's house. We always stop for food and gas at the same places. We never have to ask how much longer because we know all the markers on the highway. We see the same sights on our journeys . . . until last year. That was the year that they closed the highway, and we had to find another route. The first place we stopped was a gas station with a worn out store that had nothing but _____ _____ _____. The restroom was not even in working order! That was bad news because all the snacks in our car were ruined when my little brother _____ _____ _____. Then, when we tried to find a suitable place to eat dinner, _____ _____. Then, the worst thing happened. _____ _____ _____. Somehow, we made it to Grandma's, relieved to have lived through that adventure and hoping to never repeat it again!

This week I learned:

- how to recognize relevant ideas for narrative writing
- how to add details to make stories exciting
- how to think about sequence
- how to recognize and correct inappropriate pronoun shifts

#51529—180 Days of Writing   © Shell Education

NAME: _____ DATE: _____

Directions: Read the titles. Write reasons why each one would or would not make a good title for a narrative.

Titles	Reasons
Adventures Are Always Fun for Everyone	
The Day We Ended Up in Outer Space	
The Reasons Our Cruise Line Is the Best	
How to Plan the Most Efficient Camping Trip for Your Family	
He Never Believed He Would See the Ocean	
The Rescue Boat Adventure	

NAME: _____ **DATE:** _____

Directions: Imagine that you have just taken a trip of a lifetime. Describe the experience, including where you went and what you did.

_____

_____

_____

_____

_____

_____

_____

_____

_____

_____

_____

_____

> ## Remember!
>
> A strong narrative paragraph:
>
> - includes an introductory and a concluding sentence
> - uses sensory details to describe the experience
> - makes it sound like a story

Cursive Practice *abc*

Directions: Use cursive to write how you would feel while visiting the place you described above.

_____

_____

_____

NAME: _____ DATE: _____

Directions: Think about the transition words that can help others understand the sequence of events in your narrative. Read the ones listed below, and add four more of your own.
Then, write two sentences about an adventure using at least two of the words from the list.

TRANSITION WORDS

Then	So	_____
At first	First	_____
But then	Next	_____
Only then	Finally	_____

1. _____

   _____

   _____

2. _____

   _____

   _____

Time to Improve!

Revisit the paragraph you wrote on page 20 about a trip of a lifetime. Add transition words to your sentences to make the sequence of events clearer for the reader.

Editing

Places I Want to Go

NAME: _____ **DATE:** _____

Directions: Add the appropriate pronouns to the sentences. Be sure to avoid inappropriate pronoun shifts.

The most exciting adventure _____ ever had was when _____ visited Machu Picchu. _____ climbed and climbed until _____ feet ached at night. _____ breaths shortened as _____ ascended the mountain. _____ thought _____ would never reach the top. But finally, _____ could see the sun rise above _____ illuminating the old dwellings of people from long ago. Being so high up gave _____ the idea that _____ could see the beginning and the end of the earth.

Time to Improve!

Revisit the paragraph you wrote on page 20 about a trip of a lifetime. Edit your text to make sure that you used pronouns appropriately. If you did not use any pronouns, find places to add them to your paragraph.

Remember!

Inappropriate pronoun shifts happen when a sentence shifts between first person (*I*, *we*) to second person (*you*) or third person (*he*, *she*, *they*).

NAME: _____ **DATE:** _____

Directions: Imagine that you have just taken a trip of a lifetime. Describe the experience, including where you went and what you did.

It was a fat summer day, and we were getting ready to fly to Cholpy Island. It's an exotic place with strange creatures named cholps. Cholps live in Basmentaria. Cholps are known to have a fat reputation, but they all work off their fat. They beg other animals for food really early in the morning and eat a very early dinner. We got to the island and I saw a cholp. The cholp was eating a tree. I was confused but I kept walking. It was getting late so we at traditional cholp dinner. It was a tree. cholp island was bad.

NAME: _____   DATE:_____

Prewriting
Gods and Heroes

Directions: Place check marks in the circles that include ideas that could be found in an informative/explanatory paragraph about Greek gods and heroes.

People love reading about the Greek hero, Odysseus.

Odysseus and his men encountered the Cyclops, the one-eyed son of the god Poseidon.

My favorite goddess is Hera because she is dramatic.

Aphrodite is the beautiful goddess of love.

Poseidon is the best Greek god.

The Greeks used myths for entertainment.

Zeus is the god of the sky in Greek mythology.

Greek mythology is more interesting than Norse mythology.

The Trojan horse myth is a story about how Greek soldiers hid inside a large wooden horse.

A centaur is a mythological creature that has the upper body of a man and lower body of a horse.

NAME: _____ **DATE:** _____

Directions: Read the paragraph. Circle the main topics, and underline the supporting facts and details.

> Greek mythology is a collection of myths, or stories, from ancient times. The Greeks used mythology for several purposes. Mythology explained the religious beliefs of the ancient Greeks. The Greeks worshiped the gods, including Zeus (god of the sky), Poseidon (god of the sea), and Hades (god of the underworld). The gods spoke to the Greeks through oracles, or priests, who told them about the future. The Greeks also used myths to explain the things they did not understand about their world. For example, Pandora's Box explains how evil came into the world. Heroes emerged from many of these stories. The Greeks used myths for entertainment and performed plays about these myths in amphitheaters. One example is the journey of Odysseus from Troy to his home. In this story, he encounters a Cyclops and the Land of the Dead. But after years of trials, this hero makes it home to his wife and kingdom. Today, myths still entertain in the form of books, plays, and movies.

Cursive Practice *abc*

Directions: Use cursive to write one interesting thing you learned from the paragraph above.

_____

_____

_____

NAME: _____ **DATE:** _____

Directions: Think about how you can revise these introductory sentences to make them more appealing to readers. Write your new sentences under the examples.

1. According to Greek myths, Zeus reigns from Mount Olympus.

_____

_____

2. This paragraph will talk about Poseidon, the god of the sea.

_____

_____

3. I think Greek myths about the gods and goddesses are fun to read.

_____

_____

4. The heroes in Greek mythology make the stories interesting.

_____

_____

5. Greek mythology is a collection of myths or stories from ancient times.

_____

_____

Boost Your Learning! 🚀

To grab the attention of the reader, make your introductory sentence strong and interesting!

Example: Have you ever thought of what it would be like to be a Greek god?

NAME: _____ **DATE:** _____

Directions: Use the ∧ symbol to add commas to set apart the nonrestrictive information in the sentences. The first one is done for you.

1. The Greeks worshipped gods, including Zeus∧god of the sky.
,

2. The story of Odysseus a Greek hero who finds his way home is a very old tale.

3. Zeus the god of the sky and king of Mount Olympus is symbolized by a thunderbolt and an eagle.

4. Persephone is kidnapped by Hades also known as the god of the underworld.

5. You can identify the statues of Poseidon the god of the sea because he is often shown with a trident.

Boost Your Learning!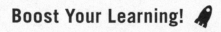

Commas can be used to add to or set apart information in a sentence. Sometimes, this information is nonrestrictive. **Nonrestrictive information** means that if we removed it from the sentence, it would not change the meaning of the sentence.

NAME: _____   DATE: _____

Directions: Revisit the paragraph. Think about how you can improve it based on what you have practiced throughout the week. Write your suggestions in the margins.

Greek mythology is a collection of myths, or stories, from ancient times. The Greeks used mythology for several purposes. Mythology explained the religious beliefs of the ancient Greeks. The Greeks worshiped the gods, including Zeus (god of the sky), Poseidon (god of the sea), and Hades (god of the underworld). The gods spoke to the Greeks through oracles, or priests, who told them about the future. The Greeks also used myths to explain the things they did not understand about their world. For example, Pandora's Box explains how evil came into the world. Heroes emerged from many of these stories. The Greeks used myths for entertainment and performed plays about these myths in amphitheaters. One example is the journey of Odysseus from Troy to his home. In this story, he encounters a Cyclops and the Land of the Dead. But after years of trials, this hero makes it home to his wife and kingdom. Today, myths still entertain in the form of books, plays, and movies.

This week I learned:

- how to develop a topic with supporting facts and examples

- how to add commas to nonrestrictive information in sentences

NAME: _____ **DATE:** _____

Directions: The ancient Greeks used myths to explain natural phenomena like seasons, earthquakes, floods, and thunderstorms. Write notes in the margins about the information you would include in an informative/explanatory paragraph about mythology and natural phenomena.

Greek myths are the best stories! They are entertaining, but these stories also give us important background information about relationships between the gods and the reasons for natural phenomena. For example, the myth involving Hades' abduction of Persephone, Demeter's daughter, tells how seasons came to be. My favorite myth is about lightning. Long ago, Greeks believed that Zeus used lightning as his weapon. Any place struck by lightning became a sacred place, and they built temples there. Earthquakes and storms happened when Poseidon, god of the sea, struck his trident to the ground in anger. A great flood happened when Zeus became irritated with humans. He and his brother, Poseidon, sent rain and flooded the earth. Sprinkled throughout these myths that explain natural phenomena are stories about how the gods treated one another. These stories make for great entertainment!

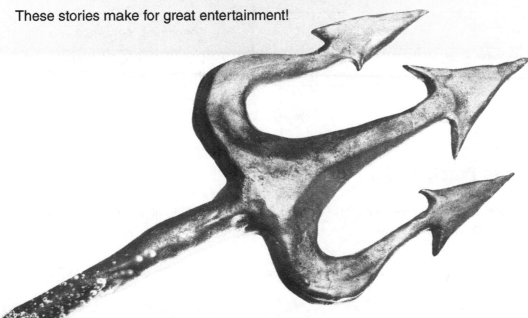

Drafting

Nature of the World

NAME: _____ **DATE:** _____

Directions: Create your own myth about a natural phenomenon. Include details about what makes the phenomenon happen. Use your notes on page 29 to help you draft your informative/explanatory paragraph.

_____

_____

_____

_____

_____

_____

_____

_____

_____

_____

_____

_____

Remember!
To draft a strong informative/explanatory paragraph, you should:
• have an introductory and a concluding sentence
• include details that support the main idea

Cursive Practice *abc*

Directions: Use cursive to explain how your new myth could fit into Greek mythology as we know it today.

_____

_____

_____

_____

NAME: _____ **DATE:** _____

Directions: A strong introduction to a paragraph gets readers interested in learning more about the topic. Explain why the introductory sentences below are interesting for readers.

1. According to Greek myths, the seasons began because Hades kidnapped Persephone and took her to the Underworld.

    _____

    _____

2. After Persephone's kidnapping, the seasons were created.

    _____

    _____

3. You hear the rumble and wonder if it might be the gods above making a statement.

    _____

    _____

4. The reason for thunder in Greek myths originates with the Cyclops hammering a thunderbolt for Zeus.

    _____

    _____

Time to Improve!

Go back to the informative/explanatory draft you wrote on page 30. Revise your introductory sentence to make sure that it grabs the attention of the reader.

NAME: _____ DATE:_____

Directions: Use the ∧ symbol to add commas to set apart the nonrestrictive information in the sentences. Then, rewrite the sentences without the information.

1. According to Greek myths seasons came to be when Persephone was

   dragged away to the underworld by Hades the god of the dead.

   _____

   _____

2. Zeus the god of the sky orders the Cyclopes to hammer lightning bolts,

   which cause earthquakes to happen.

   _____

   _____

3. Sailors rely on Poseidon the god of the sea for safe travels and

   smooth voyages.

   _____

   _____

Time to Improve!

Go back to the informative/explanatory draft you wrote on page 30. Revise at least two sentences to include nonrestrictive information.

Remember!

Nonrestrictive information means that if we removed it from the sentence, it would not change the meaning of the sentence.

NAME: _____ **DATE:** _____

Directions: Create your own myth about a natural phenomenon. Include details about what makes the phenomenon happen.

_____

_____

_____

_____

_____

_____

_____

_____

_____

_____

_____

_____

_____

_____

_____

_____

_____

_____

NAME: _____ DATE:_____

Directions: Below are some facts about original fairy tales. How can you use these facts to support the idea that fairy tales were originally written for adults? Write your notes next to each fact.

Fairy Tale Facts	Why This Is Written for Adults
Snow White orders the evil queen to wear shoes made from iron. She is ordered to dance until she drops dead.	
In the end, Hansel and Gretel kill the witch.	
In Sleeping Beauty, the prince's mother is an ogress and enjoys eating children. She almost eats her two grandchildren but is thrown in to a serpent's pit where she dies instead.	
The Frog Prince is transformed from a frog into a prince when the princess throws him to the ground.	
In the beginning of the story, Pinocchio is an ungrateful boy. When being carved, Pinocchio kicks Geppetto and runs away.	
Cinderella's stepsisters cut off parts of their feet in hopes of fitting into the golden slipper.	

NAME: _____ **DATE:** _____

Directions: Read the paragraph. Each claim should have evidence supporting it. Circle the claims and underline the evidence.

Fairy tales are stories filled with bias and violence and are better suited for adults not children. Even though the fairy tales today have been watered down from their original versions, there are still many disturbing features. For example, in the original version of Snow White, it is her biological mother who wants to kill her. Snow White is only seven years old. Does it make it any better that today's version changes this to her stepmother? This seems to show a distinct bias against stepmothers. At the end of the original story, Snow White makes the stepmother (evil queen) wear shoes made from iron. The stepmother is ordered to dance until she drops dead. In the version we know today, lightning strikes as she attempts to push a boulder onto the dwarves. Instead of killing the dwarves, she falls off a cliff to her death. Why is this a better version for children? Both versions involve a terrible death, something that is more suitable for adults. Fairy tales, both old and new, promote bias and violence. For these reasons alone, we should avoid allowing children to read fairy tales.

Boost Your Learning! 🚀

A **claim** is a statement that is argued and supported in an essay.

A claim:
- is one sentence long
- is short and to the point
- omits "I think" or "I feel"
- is defended with evidence

Revising

Fairy Tales: For Children or Adults?

NAME: _____ **DATE:** _____

Directions: Explain what each sentence means. Think about how the commas help change the meanings of the sentences.

1. The story of the poisoned apple, which is almost 200 years old, frightens young children.

   _____

   _____

2. The story of the poisoned apple which is almost 200 years old, frightens young children.

   _____

   _____

3. The Brothers Grimm fairy tales, written in the early 1800s, can be bought at bookstores today.

   _____

   _____

4. The Brothers Grimm fairy tales written in the early 1800s can be bought at bookstores today.

   _____

   _____

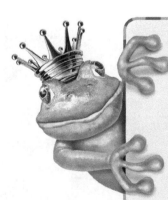

Remember!

Nonrestrictive means that if we removed it from the sentence, it would not change the meaning of the sentence. Nonrestrictive information is set off with commas. **Restrictive** means that if we removed it from the sentence, it would change the meaning of the sentence.

NAME: _____ DATE: _____

Directions: Circle the pronoun in each sentence. Then, draw an arrow from the pronoun to its antecedent.

1. The evil queen thinks she is the most beautiful in the world.

2. The witch puts Hansel and Gretel in a cage to fatten them up.

3. Cinderella is treated like a slave by her stepsisters and stepmother.

4. The Three Little Pigs are hunted down by the wolf, so they keep on running.

Boost Your Learning!

A pronoun takes the place of a noun. Pronouns have antecedents. A pronoun's **antecedent** is the word or words that the pronoun refers to or replaces.

Example: *Rapunzel* was placed in a tower so that *she* would not be found.

NAME: _____ DATE:_____

Publishing

Fairy Tales: For Children or Adults?

Directions: Revisit the paragraph. Then, answer the questions.

Fairy tales are stories filled with bias and violence and are better suited for adults not children. Even though the fairy tales today have been watered down from their original versions, there are still many disturbing features. For example, in the original version of Snow White, it is her biological mother who wants to kill her. Snow White is only seven years old. Does it make it any better that today's version changes this to her stepmother? This seems to show a distinct bias against stepmothers. At the end of the original story, Snow White makes the stepmother (evil queen) wear shoes made from iron. The stepmother is ordered to dance until she drops dead. In the version we know today, lightning strikes as she attempts to push a boulder onto the dwarves. Instead of killing the dwarves, she falls off a cliff to her death. Why is this a better version for children? Both versions involve a terrible death, something that is more suitable for adults. Fairy tales, both old and new, promote bias and violence. For these reasons alone, we should avoid allowing children to read fairy tales.

1. What is the argument the author is making?

   _____

   _____

2. Do you agree or disagree with the author's argument?

   _____

This week I learned: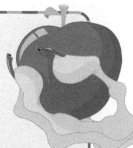

- how to use facts to support ideas
- how to look for claims in a text and identify reasons for the claims
- how to use commas to add nonrestrictive information to a sentence
- how to find a pronoun's antecedent

NAME: _____ **DATE:** _____

Directions: Free writing is a type of brainstorming. Free writing helps define perspective. Use free writing to complete the chart.

What do I know about fairy tales from the villains' perspectives?

Is it important to tell multiple perspectives? Why or why not?

NAME: _____ **DATE:** _____

Drafting

Fairy Tales: A Villain's Perspective

Directions: Do you think fairy tales would or would not be better if they were told from the villains' perspectives? Include reasons to support your argument. Use your notes from page 39 to help you draft your argument paragraph.

_____

_____

_____

_____

_____

_____

_____

_____

_____

_____

_____

_____

Remember!

A strong argument paragraph should:

• begin with an introductory sentence that states your claim

• include details that support your claim

• end with a concluding sentence

Cursive Practice *abc*

Directions: Use cursive to write how a villain might answer the question above.

_____

_____

_____

_____

NAME: _____ DATE: _____

Directions: Use the ∧ symbol to add commas to set apart nonrestrictive information to the sentences. Then, explain how adding the commas changes the meanings of the sentences.

1. The story of the Frog Prince which originally showed a very selfish and bratty princess says that they lived happily ever after.

   _____

   _____

2. The tale of the evil queen giving Snow White a poisoned apple which is almost 200 years old might be different if told from the queen's perspective.

   _____

   _____

3. The wolf originally depicted as the villain in the story paints a picture that makes the Three Little Pigs look like the true villains in the story.

   _____

   _____

Time to Improve!

Look at the draft you wrote on page 40.
Revise at least two sentences to include
nonrestrictive information.

NAME: _____ DATE: _____

Directions: Circle the pronouns. Then, draw arrows from the pronouns to their antecedents.

1. The wolf believes he is the one in the right, not the pigs.

2. The witch is only trying to cut corners when she finds Hansel and Gretel eating the house.

3. Cinderella's stepmother is only looking out for her two older daughters first.

4. The evil queen tells terrible stories of how her stepchild does not obey the rules.

· ·

Time to Improve!

Revisit the paragraph you wrote on page 40. Edit your text to make sure you used pronouns and antecedents correctly. If you can't find any, consider adding pronouns and antecedents to vary your writing.

Remember!

An antecedent is a word or words that a pronoun refers to or replaces.

NAME: _____ **DATE:** _____

Directions: Do you think fairy tales would or would not be better if they were told from the villains' perspectives? Include reasons to support your argument.

_____

_____

_____

_____

_____

_____

_____

_____

_____

_____

_____

_____

_____

_____

_____

_____

_____

_____

_____

NAME: _____   DATE: _____

Directions: Read the report about an unsolved crime. Write notes in the chart below about why each suspect may have committed the crime.

A crime occurred at the home of a famous filmmaker, Wilamena. After filming the final scenes of her latest movie, she invited two cast members over to her home. One of the guests noticed Wilamena lying unconscious on the floor around 1 A.M. This guest called the police and then disappeared from the crime scene. The emergency phone operator said the voice was deep and low. When the police arrived, they found no shoe prints or fingerprints at the scene but only chocolate on the ground. To their surprise, she suddenly woke up! Wilamena doesn't remember what happened, but she had a large bump on the very top of her head.

Suspect 1: Chet was the stunt director for Wilamena's latest film. He loves race car driving barefoot. Chet's left hand is deformed and he often wears a glove to cover it. The police found out that Chet was mad because Wilamena cut some of his greatest stunts from the movie.

Suspect 2: Ginger is a historian who knows everything about the history in the movie. Wilamena could not have produced the movie without her. Most of the time, Ginger snacks on sweets such as chocolate. The police found out that Wilamena had yelled at Ginger for eating all her chocolate.

Claim	Evidence
1. Ginger committed the crime.	
2. Chet committed the crime.	

NAME: _____ **DATE:**_____

Directions: Read the paragraphs. Circle the claim in each one. Underline the parts of the paragraphs that support the claims. Then, answer the question.

Paragraph 1

Suspect 1, Chet, committed the crime. He was clearly the one who called the police since the operator said the voice was deep and low. Also, the police found out that Chet was mad at Wilamena because she cut some of his greatest stunts from the movie. He also wears a glove to cover his hand, which could be why there were no fingerprints at the scene. There is no doubt that Chet committed the crime.

Paragraph 2

Suspect 2, Ginger, committed the crime. Although Wilamena could not have produced this latest movie without Ginger, she was upset with Ginger and yelled at her in front of everyone on set because she ate all of her chocolate. Lastly, chocolate was found on the floor of the crime scene. Clearly, Ginger committed the crime.

1. Which paragraph makes the stronger claim? Explain why.

_____

_____

_____

_____

_____

Cursive Practice *abc*

Directions: Who do you think committed this crime? Use cursive to write your answer.

_____

NAME: _____ DATE: _____

Directions: Circle the possessive pronouns in the sentences. Then, explain how each pronoun shows ownership.

1. Chet races his cars barefoot.

   _____

   _____

2. Wilamena humiliates Ginger after Ginger eats her chocolate.

   _____

   _____

3. Ginger's specialty is her knowledge of history.

   _____

   _____

4. The police use their evidence to solve the crime.

   _____

   _____

Boost Your Learning!

A **possessive pronoun** is a pronoun that shows ownership of something.

Example: Wilamena filmed *her* ideas. This shows that the ideas belong to Wilamena.

NAME: _____ DATE:_____

Directions: Use the ℒ symbol to replace the underlined nouns with possessive pronouns.

1. Her
   Wilamena's voice was loud when she embarrassed Ginger.

2. Ginger's specialty was history.

3. On the speedway, Chet's racecar is lightning fast.

4. The police wondered how Wilamena's head got that bump.

5. Everyone heard the complaints about Wilamena's chocolate.

Boost Your Learning! 🚀

Possessive pronouns never use apostrophes.

Correct: its   yours   hers

Incorrect: it's   your's   her's

NAME: _____ DATE:_____

Publishing

Unsolved Mysteries

Directions: Reread the paragraphs. Write notes in the margins next to each one about what the author could add in order to make them stronger.

Paragraph 1

Suspect 1, Chet, committed the crime. He was clearly the one who called the police since the operator said the voice was deep and low. Also, the police found out that Chet was mad at Wilamena because she cut some of his greatest stunts from the movie. He also wears a glove to cover his hand, which could be why there were no fingerprints at the scene. There is no doubt that Chet committed the crime.

Paragraph 2

Suspect 2, Ginger, committed the crime. Although Wilamena could not have produced this latest movie without Ginger, she was upset with Ginger and yelled at her in front of everyone on set because she ate all of her chocolate. Lastly, chocolate was found on the floor of the crime scene. Clearly, Ginger committed the crime.

This week I learned:

- how to select relevant information in a text
- how to support claims with evidence
- how to identify possessive pronouns

EVIDENCE IDENTIFICATION

NAME: _____ DATE: _____

Directions: Read the scenario about a supposed ghost story. Underline the relevant information that could lead to solving the mystery. Then, form an argument to support the idea that a ghost delivered the cupcake and an argument that does not support the idea.

It was the year that my pet dog, Rosebud, died in an accident. Instead of sleepwalking, which used to be a problem for me, I began having nightmares. My birthday was coming up, and I dreaded the celebration because she would not be there. The night before my birthday, I dreamed that she visited me in my room. She brought a cupcake frosted with my favorite color, pink. She told me to not worry about her. She had found peace, and she wanted me to enjoy my day because her spirit would be with me celebrating the day. I woke suddenly and found that my hands and face were spattered with something sweet. Flour paw prints covered the floor. Then, I saw the cupcake on my table. It was the exact cupcake in my dream. She must have visited me after all.

Support	Does Not Support

Drafting | Ghosts

NAME: _____ **DATE:** _____

Directions: Do you think a ghost delivered the cupcake in the story on page 49? Use details to support your argument. Use your notes to help you draft your argument paragraph.

_____

_____

_____

_____

_____

_____

_____

_____

_____

_____

_____

_____

Remember!

A strong argument paragraph should:

* begin with an introductory sentence that states your claim

* include details that support your claim

* end with a concluding sentence

Cursive Practice *abc*

Directions: Use cursive to explain why you do or do not believe in ghosts.

_____

_____

_____

_____

NAME: _____ **DATE:** _____

Directions: Circle the possessive pronouns in the story. Then, underline the objects that they show ownership of in the sentences.

Example: The twin sister baked (her) cupcake.

It was the year that my pet dog, Rosebud, died in an accident. Instead of sleepwalking, which used to be a problem for me, I began having nightmares. My birthday was coming up and I dreaded the celebration because she would not be there. The night before my birthday, I dreamed that she visited me in my room. She brought a cupcake frosted with my favorite color, pink. She told me to not worry about her. She had found peace, and she wanted me to enjoy my day because her spirit would be with me celebrating the day. I woke suddenly and found that my hands and face were spattered with something sweet. Flour paw prints covered the floor. Then, I saw the cupcake on my table. It was the exact cupcake in my dream. She must have visited me after all.

Boost Your Learning! 🚀

A **possessive pronoun** possesses or shows ownership of something. *Her* cupcake is pink. *Her* possesses or owns the cupcake.

Editing

Ghosts

NAME: _____ **DATE:** _____

Directions: Use the ℒ symbol to replace the underlined noun in each sentence with a possessive pronoun. Then, explain why the pronoun is possessive.

1. <u>Kara's</u> specialty was making cupcakes.

_____

_____

2. In her dreams, <u>Rosebud's</u> memory seemed so real.

_____

_____

3. Kara wondered how <u>Rosebud's</u> cupcake landed on her table.

_____

_____

4. Everyone wondered about the mess on <u>Kara's</u> face, hands, and floor.

_____

_____

· ·

Time to Improve!

Revisit the claims and evidence you drafted on page 50. Edit your writing to add in more possessive pronouns.

NAME: _____ **DATE:** _____

Directions: Do you think a ghost delivered the cupcake in the story on page 49? Use details to support your argument.

_____

_____

_____

_____

_____

_____

_____

_____

_____

_____

_____

_____

_____

_____

_____

_____

_____

_____

NAME: _____ **DATE:** _____

Directions: Below are facts about how royalty lived in medieval times. Use the facts to write two lines of dialogue (one per person) between two people living in that situation. The first one is done for you.

Royalty Facts	My Dialogue
After hunting season, nobles spent time feasting and gambling.	"Did you see my catch of the day? It's huge!" "I did see it! I bet you're ready to eat after such a big catch."
Noble children were sent to be apprentices at the castle.	
These children worked as pages, squires, knights, and maids of honor.	
Ladies of the castle spent time managing the workers of the castle.	
Once things were taken care of, the ladies spent their afternoon doing needlework.	
After dinner, the people enjoyed entertainment of music, jugglers, dancing, and plays.	

NAME: _____ DATE:_____

Directions: Read the paragraph. Find places where dialogue could be added. Add notes in the margins about what the dialogue should be.

The shaking peasant approached the lord. The lord asked why he was shaking. The peasant told him that he did not pay his tithe to the church that year. The lord asked why he didn't fulfill the obligations since it only required 10 percent of his crops. The peasant replied, "I knew my family would not have enough food to eat, so I did not pay." He continued to explain that he knew the church's tithe barn was overflowing. The lord reminded him that this debt would be written down in the Domesday Book.

· ·

Cursive Practice *abc*

Directions: Use cursive to write at least three sentences that tell how it would feel to be the peasant in the above scenario.

_____

_____

_____

_____

Revising

Living as Royalty

NAME: _____ **DATE:** _____

Directions: Circle the pronouns in the sentences. Then, write *S* for subjective or *O* for objective before each sentence to show the case of the pronoun.

Case	Explanations	Example
subjective	The **subjective case** is used when the pronoun is the subject of the sentence.	**She** attended to the duties of the castle.
objective	The **objective case** is used when the pronoun is the object of a verb or preposition.	The lord of the castle gave **him** orders for the day.

_____**1.** Life in the castle was busy for its inhabitants.

_____**2.** In the morning, he heard the report about the crops.

_____**3.** When the work was sloppy, the lady of the castle treated him harshly.

_____**4.** Later in the day, he hunted with the men.

_____**5.** They retired for bed when the lord was tired.

Boost Your Learning! 🚀

I, *you*, *he*, *she*, *it*, *we*, and *they* are subject pronouns.

Me, *you*, *him*, *her*, *it*, *us*, and *them* are object pronouns because they receive the action of the verb.

NAME: _____ DATE:_____

Directions: Use the ✐ symbol to replace the underlined parts in each sentence with a pronoun. Then, write *S* for subjective or *O* for objective on the lines.

_____1. <u>The knight</u> served the lord of the castle by fighting.

_____2. At just seven years old, <u>the page</u> had to wait tables and help the lord dress for the day.

_____3. The castle served as a school for the the <u>knights</u>.

_____4. After serving for seven years, <u>squires</u> became knights and learned how to defend the lord.

Boost Your Learning! 🚀

Be aware of incorrect uses of pronouns!

Example: The lord and me took care of granting permission for marriages.

NAME: _____ **DATE:** _____

Directions: Revisit the paragraph. Then, answer the questions.

The shaking peasant approached the lord. The lord asked why he was shaking. The peasant told him that he did not pay his tithe to the church that year. The lord asked why he didn't fulfill the obligations since it only required 10 percent of his crops. The peasant replied, "I knew my family would not have enough food to eat, so I did not pay." He continued to explain that he knew the church's tithe barn was overflowing. The lord reminded him that this debt would be written down in the Domesday Book.

1. What makes this a narrative?

_____

_____

_____

2. Is there anything the author could improve on?

_____

_____

_____

This week I learned: 🖊📓

- how to add dialogue to narratives
- how to identify subjective and objective pronouns

NAME: _____ DATE: _____

Directions: Below are some facts about how peasants lived in medieval times. Use these facts to write dialogue between two peasants living back then.

Peasant Facts	My Dialogue
Peasants built homes using mud, straw, and manure while the lords lived in castles.	
The priest required that the peasants work the church land for free.	
Peasant children did not go to school; instead they worked in the fields.	
After paying taxes to the lords and church, the peasants often did not have enough to feed their families.	

Drafting
Living as Peasants

NAME: _____ **DATE:** _____

Directions: Imagine you are a peasant living during the medieval time period. Describe one day, including who you speak with and the events that take place. Use the facts and dialogue from page 59 to help you draft your narrative paragraph.

_____

_____

_____

_____

_____

_____

_____

_____

_____

_____

_____

_____

_____

_____

> **Remember!**
>
> A strong narrative paragraph:
>
> • includes an introductory and a concluding sentence
>
> • uses sensory details to describe the experience
>
> • makes it sound like a story

Cursive Practice *abc*

Directions: Use cursive to write a title for your narrative.

_____

_____

NAME: _____ DATE: _____

Directions: Circle the correct pronoun in each sentence. Then, write *S* if it is subjective or *O* if it is objective.

_____1. They/Them built homes from mud, straw, and manure.

_____2. The priest required they/them to work the church land for free.

_____3. Life as a peasant was hard for they/them.

_____4. A peasant's family sometimes went hungry when they/them had to pay tax.

_____5. Instead of going to school, he/him worked in the family field.

. . . .

Time to Improve!

Write two sentences using objective and subjective case pronouns.

Remember!

The subjective case is used when the pronoun is the subject of a sentence. The objective case is used when the pronoun is the object of a verb or preposition.

NAME: _____ **DATE:** _____

Directions: Use the facts to write two sentences that have subjective case pronouns. Then, write two sentences that have objective case pronouns.

Facts

Peasant families all slept in the same room together.

Peasant children did not attend school.

Children cleared stones off the land and chased birds away from the fields.

Life was hard for peasants.

1. _____

_____

2. _____

_____

3. _____

_____

4. _____

_____

Remember!

To tell the difference between a subjective or objective pronoun, first decide if it acts as the subject of the sentence. If so, it is a subjective pronoun. If it receives the action of the verb, then it is an objective pronoun.

NAME: _____ **DATE:** _____

Directions: Imagine you are a peasant living during the medieval time period. Describe one day, including whom you speak with and the events that take place.

NAME: _____ **DATE:** _____

Directions: Place check marks in the circles with information you could use in a narrative paragraph about Renaissance artists. Give reasons for your answers under the information.

Michelangelo remembered the misery he felt painting the Sistine Chapel.

Rumor has it that Michelangelo and Leonardo da Vinci were competitors and did not like one another.

While painting *The Last Supper*, Leonardo da Vinci experimented with painting on dry plaster.

Renaissance Artists

Some people argue about who was the greatest Renaissance artist of all time.

The *Mona Lisa* is my most favorite painting in the world!

NAME: _____ DATE: _____

Directions: Read the paragraph. Find places where more detail and description could be added. Add ideas in the margins about what the descriptions could be.

It had been 20 years since Michelangelo had painted the ceiling. He arrived back at the chapel and took in the beauty of its scenes. He saw the creation of Adam, the creation of Eve, and the flood of Noah. He remembered the misery he felt painting during those long four years. How his body had hurt, and how much he complained!

When he had first received the commission by the Pope to paint the ceiling, he had been sculpting an art piece. "I'm a sculptor not a painter!" Michelangelo wanted to finish the tomb. But the Pope is the Pope, and it was useless to fight the order.

Now, Michelangelo stands and looks at a wall that will be the canvas for his next painting, *The Last Judgment*. Now that he is older, he wonders how long it will take to complete this painting.

Cursive Practice 𝒶𝒷𝒸

Directions: Write a sentence in cursive that tells how Michelangelo felt about painting the ceiling of the Sistine Chapel.

_____

_____

Revising

Renaissance Artists

NAME: _____ **DATE:** _____

Directions: Rewrite the paragraph using varied sentence length. Use pages 64 and 65 to help you add details.

> Leonardo da Vinci painted *The Last Supper* on the walls of a dining hall in a monastery. Instead of painting on wet plaster, he painted directly on the wall, which caused the painting to deteriorate quickly. Over the years, people have tried to restore the painting back to its original condition. The last restoration took place in 1978 and took 20 years to complete.

_____

_____

_____

_____

_____

_____

_____

_____

_____

Boost Your Learning!

To vary sentence length, make one sentence longer with more details. Follow that sentence with a shorter sentence that is more direct and to the point.

Example: Leonardo da Vinci lived during the exciting time of the Renaissance and worked as an artist, inventor, scientist, author, architect, and engineer. In truth, he was a Renaissance man.

NAME: _____ DATE: _____

Editing

Renaissance Artists

Directions: Use the ∧ symbol to add commas to set off the nonrestrictive information in the sentences. Then, write your own sentence with nonrestrictive information.

1. *Mona Lisa* Leonardo da Vinci's most famous painting is housed in the Louvre in Paris, France.

2. Michelangelo wrote a poem about his work in the Sistine Chapel something that was very unpleasant for him.

3. Patrons hired artists such as Leonardo da Vinci and Michelangelo to paint and sculpt works of art.

4. The sculpture of *David* is out of proportion something Michelangelo did on purpose but still commands awe from viewers.

5. _____

   _____

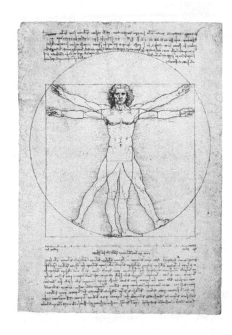

NAME: _____ **DATE:** _____

Directions: Revisit the paragraph. Then, answer the questions.

It had been 20 years since Michelangelo had painted the ceiling. He arrived back at the chapel and took in the beauty of its scenes. He saw the creation of Adam, the creation of Eve, and the flood of Noah. He remembered the misery he felt painting during those long four years. How his body had hurt, and how much he complained!

When he first received the commission, he had been sculpting a tomb for the pope. "I'm a sculptor not a painter!" Michelangelo wanted to finish the tomb. But the Pope is the Pope and it was useless to fight the order.

Michelangelo stood there and looked at the wall that would be the canvas for his next painting, *The Last Judgement.* Now that he was older, he wondered how long it would take to complete this painting.

1. What makes this a strong narrative?

   _____

   _____

   _____

2. Give two examples of how the author uses nonrestrictive information.

   _____

   _____

   _____

This week I learned:

- how to add detail and description to narratives
- how to set apart nonrestrictive information using commas
- how to vary sentence length to make narratives more interesting

NAME: _____ **DATE:** _____

Directions: Based on the topics in the chart, what are some ideas for narratives? Write your ideas in the right column.

Topics	Ideas for Narratives
Leonardo da Vinci developed the idea of the submarine.	
Johannes Gutenberg invented the first printing press.	
Galileo Galilei used the telescope to study the heavens.	
Filippo Brunelleschi invented the mechanical clock.	
Sir John Harrington created the first flush toilet for Queen Elizabeth.	

Drafting

Renaissance Inventions

NAME: _____ **DATE:** _____

Directions: Imagine you are living during the Renaissance. Write about a Renaissance invention, and describe how it can change the way people live or learn. Then, use one of the topics and your notes from page 69 to help you draft a narrative paragraph.

_____

_____

_____

_____

_____

_____

_____

_____

_____

_____

_____

_____

_____

_____

Remember!

A strong narrative paragraph:

- includes an introductory and a concluding sentence

- uses sensory details to describe the experience

- makes it sound like a story

Cursive Practice *abc*

Directions: Use cursive to write a sentence about which Renaissance invention you think is the most important.

_____

_____

NAME: _____ **DATE:** _____

Directions: Rewrite the paragraph using varied sentence lengths.

Before the invention of the printing press, it could take months or years for monks to painstakingly copy each book by hand. Because of this long process, books were expensive to buy for the common man. Johannes Gutenberg, a German goldsmith, took things that were already invented, such as ink, paper, moveable type, and a press and combined them. What he came up with was a printing press that made books much cheaper and quicker to reproduce.

_____

_____

_____

_____

_____

_____

_____

_____

_____

_____

_____

Boost Your Learning! 🚀

Another way to vary sentences is to change the way each sentence begins. For example, make sure each sentence does not start with *The.*

Editing
Renaissance Inventions

NAME: _____ **DATE:** _____

Directions: Use the ∧ symbol to add commas to set off the nonrestrictive information in the sentences. Then, write your own sentence with nonrestrictive information.

1. The flush toilet invented by Sir John Harrington was created for Queen Elizabeth in her castle.

2. Johannes Gutenberg combined ink, paper, moveable type, and a press to create the first printing press something that has changed book making forever.

3. Galileo Galilei a scientist during the Renaissance used the telescope to study the heavens and wrote about his findings in his book, *Starry Messenger*.

4. The dome of the cathedral a beautiful building in Italy was engineered by the architect Filippo Brunelleschi.

5. _____

_____

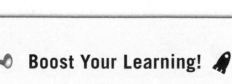

Boost Your Learning! 🚀

Nonrestrictive information can be added to sentences using commas, parentheses, and dashes.

NAME: _____ **DATE:** _____

Directions: Imagine you are living during the Renaissance. Write about a Renaissance invention, and describe how it can change the way people live or learn.

_____

_____

_____

_____

_____

_____

_____

_____

_____

_____

_____

_____

_____

_____

_____

_____

_____

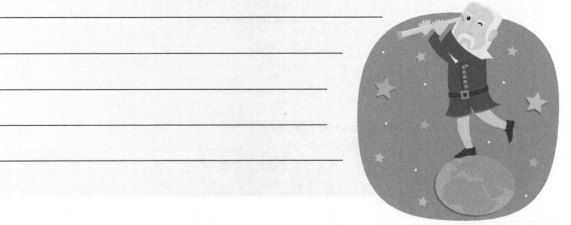

NAME: _____ DATE:_____

Directions: What questions would you ask the following people about their lives as pirates to include in a narrative paragraph? Fill in the chart with your questions.

Pirate Facts	Questions
Sir Francis Drake is best known as the Queen's privateer because he secretly stole from Spanish ships.	
Blackbeard was only a pirate for two years, but he was the most popular pirate in the Caribbean.	
The Scottish sea captain, William Kidd, was put on trial and executed for piracy.	
The female pirate, Mary Read, often dressed as a man and patrolled the waters of the Caribbean.	
Pirate Edward England popularized the Jolly Roger flag and spared the captains of the ships he captured.	

NAME: _____ **DATE:** _____

Directions: Read the narrative paragraph about Mary Reed. Write notes in the margins about where the author could include more details to make the paragraph more exciting.

Mary Read is one of the most famous female pirates of the 1700s. But, she never really planned on being a pirate. After her husband died, she joined the army and boarded a ship. When a pirate captured her ship, he kept her as a crew member. After a while, she found that she enjoyed the pirate life. From then on, she dressed as a man and patrolled the waters of the Caribbean.

Remember!

When writing narrative paragraphs, focus on one event. For example, instead of trying to tell an entire story in a paragraph, only tell one brief snapshot about the event.

Cursive Practice _abc_

Directions: Use cursive to write a sentence explaining what you would do if you were a pirate.

_____

_____

_____

Revising

Pirates and Treasures

NAME: _____ **DATE:** _____

Directions: Read the sentences. Then, revise them to vary the sentence openings.

1. Blackbeard's actual name was Edward Teach. Blackbeard was only a pirate for three years but is probably the most famous pirate in history.

   _____

   _____

   _____

2. Sir Francis Drake worked as a pirate against the Spanish ships. Drake was nicknamed the Queen's Pirate because he worked for Queen Elizabeth.

   _____

   _____

   _____

3. William Kidd had some skirmishes at sea and was named a pirate. Kidd was put on trial and executed for being a pirate.

   _____

   _____

   _____

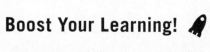

Boost Your Learning!

To make narratives more interesting for readers, vary the sentence openings.

Examples

- Blackbeard was one of the most popular pirates in history.

- Known for his great treasures, Blackbeard gained popularity as a pirate.

NAME: _____ DATE: _____

Directions: Use the ℓ symbol to replace the underlined words with more descriptive actions.

1. During battle, Blackbeard <u>scared</u> his enemies by burning fuses in his beard to create a smoke effect.

2. Instead of gold, Blackbeard <u>found</u> treasure such as barrels of sugar and cocoa.

3. Legends say that Blackbeard's body <u>went</u> around the ship three times after he was killed and thrown overboard.

4. Some <u>say</u> that Blackbeard was the most successful pirate, but that is simply not true.

Boost Your Learning! 🚀

A thesaurus is a resource that can help add more descriptive actions to your narrative.

Publishing

Pirates and Treasures

NAME: _____ DATE: _____

Directions: Revisit the narrative paragraph. Add details to the paragraph to make it more exciting. Then, answer the question.

> Mary Read is one of the most famous female pirates of the 1700s. But, she never really planned on being a pirate. _____ _____ _____. After her husband died, she joined the army and boarded a ship. _____ _____ _____. When a pirate captured her ship, he kept her as a crew member. _____ _____ _____. After a while, she found that she enjoyed the pirate life. _____ _____ _____. From then on, she dressed as a man and patrolled the waters of the Caribbean.

1. How did your details add to the story?

_____

_____

_____

This week I learned:

- how to focus on one event in narrative paragraphs
- how to vary sentence openings to make narratives more interesting
- how to add descriptive action words to narratives

NAME: _____ DATE: _____

Directions: What questions would you ask the following people about their lives as explorers to include in a narrative paragraph? Then, imagine you are an explorer and write notes about adventures you want to embark on.

Explorer Facts	Questions
Christopher Columbus wanted to sail west in hopes of reaching the Spice Islands. He first asked the king of Portugal for help, and he refused, but the queen of Spain sent him on this journey.	
Amerigo Vespucci explored America in the late 1490s and later, German mapmaker named the new land, America, after him.	
Ferdinand Magellan's crew was the first to sail around the world, but Magellan was killed in a fight when they landed on the Philippines.	
Hérnan Cortés tricked the Aztec ruler Moctezuma and defeated the Aztec empire, stealing all their gold and riches.	

My Adventure

NAME: _____ DATE: _____

Directions: Imagine you are an explorer. Draft a narrative that describes your adventure and what you discovered. Use your notes from page 79 to help you draft your paragraph.

_____

_____

_____

_____

_____

_____

_____

_____

_____

_____

_____

_____

_____

_____

Remember!

A strong narrative paragraph:

- includes an introductory and a concluding sentence

- uses sensory details to describe the experience

- makes it sound like a story

Cursive Practice *abc*

Directions: Use cursive to explain why you think going on an adventure is important.

_____

_____

_____

NAME: _____ **DATE:** _____

Directions: Read the sentences. Rewrite them using varied openings to make them more interesting.

1. Christopher Columbus sailed across the ocean hoping to find the Far East. Columbus reached North America instead.

_____

_____

_____

2. Ferdinand Magellan's crew was the first to circumnavigate the earth. Magellan actually died during the journey, but his crew sailed on.

_____

_____

_____

3. Amerigo Vespucci discovered South America on his journey. Vespucci was given the honor of having the Americas named after him.

_____

_____

_____

Boost Your Learning!

Sometimes when varying the opening of the sentence, the entire structure of the sentence changes.

Example
Captain Cook cured his crew of scurvy by giving them fresh fruit.

Out of concern for his men, Captain John Cook ordered them to eat fresh fruit and ended up curing them of scurvy.

Time to Improve!

Revisit the paragraph you wrote on page 80 about an adventure into the unknown. Add varied sentence openings to make your paragraph more interesting.

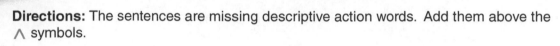

NAME: _____ **DATE:** _____

Editing

Adventures into the Unknown

Directions: The sentences are missing descriptive action words. Add them above the ∧ symbols.

1. Columbus ∧ the king of Portugal to fund an expedition.

2. The queen ∧ explorers, and so she gave Columbus the money and three ships to explore the uncharted waters.

3. Columbus ∧ where he landed was near India, so he called the natives *Indians*.

4. In all, Columbus ∧ four times to the New World.

Boost Your Learning!

To make writing interesting, be descriptive about actions in a narrative. Don't say: *Columbus found the New World and said it was the Spice Islands.* Instead say: *Columbus discovered the New World and believed it was the Spice Islands.*

Time to Improve!

Revisit the paragraph you wrote on page 80 about an adventure into the unknown. Edit your text to make sure you include descriptive action words. If you did not use any descriptive action words, find places to add them.

© Shell Education

NAME: _____ **DATE:** _____

Directions: Imagine you are an explorer. Write a narrative that describes your adventure and what you discovered.

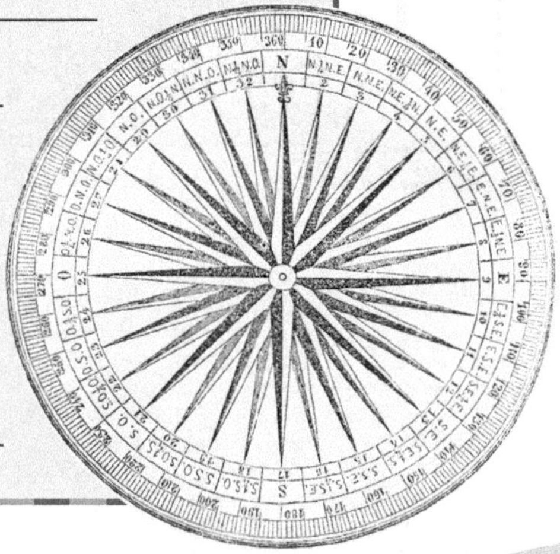

_____

_____

_____

_____

_____

_____

_____

_____

_____

_____

_____

_____

_____

_____

_____

_____

_____

_____

_____

NAME: _____ **DATE:** _____

Directions: Look at the pictures of the bridges. Then, answer the question.

Suspension Bridge

Arch Bridge

1. How are these bridges similar and different?

   _____

   _____

   _____

NAME: _____ **DATE:** _____

Directions: Read the informative/explanatory paragraph. Label each sentence as *exclamatory* (E), *interrogative* (IN), *imperative* (IM), or *declarative* (D). The first one is done for you.

___E___ What amazing structures bridges are! _____You may have noticed that bridges often look different from one another. _____Engineers build four main types of bridges: beam bridges, truss bridges, arch bridges, and suspension bridges. _____They have a few things to consider when deciding which type to build. _____What kinds of materials are available? _____How long does the bridge need to be? _____The answers to these questions help them decide on the shape, size, and type of bridge that they will build. _____The next time you cross a bridge, pause for a moment and think about what went into building it.

Boost Your Learning! 🚀

To make your writing more interesting, vary the types of sentences you use.

- **Exclamatory sentences** express strong emotion and end with exclamation points.
- **Imperative sentences** give commands and can end with periods or exclamation points.
- **Interrogative sentences** ask questions and end with question marks.
- **Declarative sentences** make statements and end with periods.

Cursive Practice

Directions: Use cursive to write a sentence explaining why bridges are important.

_____

_____

Revising

Building Bridges

NAME: _____ DATE: _____

Directions: Follow the directions to change the declarative sentences.

1. Change this sentence to an imperative sentence:
Engineers have a few things to consider when deciding which type of bridge to build.

_____

_____

_____

2. Change this sentence to an exclamatory sentence:
Bridges often look different from one another.

_____

_____

_____

3. Change this sentence to an interrogative sentence:
Engineers decide on the shape, size, and type of bridge that they will build.

_____

_____

_____

Remember!

Don't go overboard when changing the sentence structure. Change only a few sentences to make your writing stronger.

NAME: _____ **DATE:** _____

Directions: Some information is necessary to understand sentences. Use the ∧ symbol to add correct punctuation and the ≡ symbol to correct the capitalization errors.

1. Most beam bridges are less than 250 feet (76 meters) long a beam bridge looks like a long, straight line the beam is heavy so it has to be a shorter bridge otherwise, it will collapse

2. The bridge that can span the farthest is the suspension bridge a suspension bridge is suspended in air by cables

3. The bridge with the most strength is the arch bridge arch bridges can carry the most weight because of the design of the arch long ago the Romans used these types of bridges

4. Perhaps the most complex bridge is the truss bridge a truss bridge is a bridge supported by frames of beams in a triangular shape these trusses work together to hold up the bridge

Boost Your Learning! 🚀

Topic sentences need details. When writing informative/ explanatory paragraphs, be sure to include explanations and definitions so that readers can understand your topic. For example, a paragraph on bridges needs to not only list the types of bridges but also define the distinct characteristics of the bridges for the reader.

NAME: _____ DATE:_____

Directions: Read the informative/explanatory paragraph. Then, answer the questions.

Bridges often look different from one another. Engineers build four main types of bridges: beam bridges, truss bridges, arch bridges, and suspension bridges. They have a few things to consider when deciding which type to build. They think about the materials that are available. They think about how long the bridge needs to be. Answering these thoughts helps them decide on the shape, size, and type of bridge that they will build. Bridges are amazing structures.

1. What makes this a strong informative/explanatory paragraph?

_____

_____

_____

_____

2. What advice would you give the author to improve the paragraph?

_____

_____

_____

_____

NAME: _____ DATE: _____

Directions: Look at the pictures of different types of parachutes and read their descriptions. Then, answer the questions.

Round Parachute

Cargo can be heavy, so a round parachute is used because the shape offers the most drag.

Ribbon-Ring Parachute

To keep from breaking, ribbon-ring parachutes have openings that allow air to pass through.

Ram-Air Parachute

Ram-air parachutes spread out and allow for more control of both the speed and direction.

Square Parachute

Skydivers prefer square parachutes because the shape reduces swinging movements.

1. Which parachute do you think is most important? Explain why?

_____

_____

_____

_____

Drafting

Designing Parachutes

NAME: _____   **DATE:** _____

Directions: Explain the differences between round, ribbon-ring, ram-air, and square parachutes. Use your notes from page 89 to help you draft your informative/explanatory paragraph.

_____

_____

_____

_____

_____

_____

_____

_____

_____

_____

_____

_____

_____

_____

> **Remember!**
>
> To draft a strong informative/explanatory paragraph, you should:
>
> - have an introductory and a concluding sentence
>
> - include details that support the main idea

Cursive Practice *abc*

Directions: Use cursive to write a sentence explaining why parachutes are important.

_____

_____

_____

NAME: _____ **DATE:** _____

Directions: Follow the directions to change the declarative sentences.

1. Change this sentence to an imperative sentence and then an exclamatory sentence.
   To keep a parachute from breaking while falling at a fast speed, someone might use a ribbon-ring parachute.

   Imperative sentence _____

   _____

   Exclamatory sentence _____

   _____

2. Change this sentence to an exclamatory sentence and then an interrogative sentence.
   The force of the air does not break the parachute.

   Exclamatory sentence _____

   _____

   Interrogative sentence _____

   _____

3. Change this sentence to an interrogative sentence and then an imperative sentence.
   There are many different types of parachutes.

   Interrogative sentence _____

   _____

   Imperative sentence _____

   _____

 Boost Your Learning!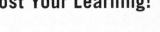

When changing sentences in a piece of writing, don't make all the sentences interrogative. Asking too many questions of the reader can wear them out!

Editing

Designing Parachutes

NAME: _____ **DATE:** _____

Directions: Some information is necessary to understand the sentences. Use the ∧ symbol to add correct punctuation and use the ≡ symbol to correct the capitalization errors.

1. Skydivers prefer square parachutes the shape reduces swinging movements

2. Ram-air parachutes help control speed and direction so, this makes them ideal for people needing to land in particular places and at controlled speeds the force of the air does not break the ram-air parachute

3. Ribbon-ring parachutes have openings that allow air to pass through this keeps the parachute from breaking even if it is traveling at a high speed

4. Cargo can be heavy so a round parachute is used because the shape offers the most drag this way the cargo does not drop at a high speed and can land safely

Boost Your Learning!

Be sure to give enough information about a topic so readers can make sense of the paragraph. For example, a paragraph on parachutes needs to not only list the types of parachutes, but also define the characteristics of them for the reader.

NAME: _____ **DATE:** _____

Directions: Explain the differences between round, ribbon-ring, ram-air, and square parachutes.

_____
_____
_____
_____
_____
_____
_____
_____
_____
_____
_____
_____
_____
_____
_____
_____
_____
_____

NAME: _____ DATE:_____

Prewriting

Groundhog Day

Directions: Place check marks in the circles with ideas that you would include in an argument paragraph about Groundhog Day.

People should not celebrate Groundhog Day because it is not as important of a day compared to other holidays.

I think Groundhog Day should be celebrated because it is a fun day that brings people together.

Should We Celebrate Groundhog Day?

Groundhog Day should be celebrated because most students like to learn about groundhogs and the weather during that time of year.

Groundhog Day should be celebrated because it is a German tradition that has been around for hundreds of years.

Groundhog Day should not be celebrated because it is not an accurate way to predict the weather.

NAME: _____ DATE: _____

Directions: Read the argument paragraph. Write notes in the margins about how the author can make her argument stronger.

Some people wonder if Groundhog Day is a holiday worth celebrating. Groundhog Day falls halfway between the winter solstice and the spring equinox. In the 1700s, German settlers made their way to Pennsylvania. They brought with them folklore involving hibernating animals as a way to predict the weather for that year. According to superstition, the sun caused the groundhog to see his shadow. The shadow would frighten the groundhog back into hibernation. They interpreted this to mean the remainder of their winter would be cold and stormy. On the other hand, if it were cloudy, the groundhog would not be frightened back into hibernation. This meant that spring would come early. Many of the German settlers were farmers. They used this information for planting crops. By 1887, the local newspaper promoted the groundhog as the official weather forecaster. Based on today's records, scientists say that the groundhog is only 36 percent accurate in predicting weather.

Cursive Practice *abc*

Directions: Use cursive to write a sentence explaining whether or not we should celebrate Groundhog Day.

_____

_____

Revising
Groundhog Day

NAME: _____ DATE: _____

Directions: Read the claims. Think about how you can revise them to make them better. Then, rewrite the updated versions.

1. I think that Groundhog Day should be celebrated as an official holiday because it is a tradition from settlers long ago and brings attention to the groundhog.

   _____

   _____

   _____

2. I believe that some people say Groundhog Day should be celebrated as an official holiday and others disagree.

   _____

   _____

   _____

3. Groundhog Day is not an official holiday because it is not based on truth or science but rather a tradition from long ago.

   _____

   _____

   _____

Remember!

A claim is a statement that is argued and supported in an essay.

A claim:

- is one sentence long
- is short and to the point
- omits "I think" or "I feel"
- is defended with evidence

NAME: _____ DATE: _____

Directions: Read the paragraph. There are commas missing. Use the ∧ symbol to add them.

   According to superstition the sun caused the groundhog to see his shadow and the shadow would frighten the groundhog back into hibernation. If it were cloudy then the groundhog would not be frightened back into hibernation. Spring would come early. Farmers depended on this information to plant crops. However the groundhog was not always accurate in predicting the weather. This caused many farmers to lose their crops and many of them went broke.

Boost Your Learning! 🚀

Commas can be tricky! Always include commas after introductory phrases and in compound sentences.

Examples
Introductory Phrase: In the 1700s, German settlers made their way to Pennsylvania.

Compound Sentence: The groundhog began hibernating, and the people cheered for an early spring.

NAME: _____

DATE: _____

Directions: Revisit the paragraph. Write notes about how to improve it on the lines below.

Some people wonder if Groundhog Day is a holiday worth celebrating. In the 1700s, German settlers made their way to Pennsylvania. They brought with them folklore involving hibernating animals as a way to predict the weather for that year. According to superstition, the sun caused the groundhog to see his shadow. The shadow would frighten the groundhog back into hibernation. They interpreted this to mean the remainder of their winter would be cold and stormy. On the other hand, if it were cloudy, the groundhog would not be frightened back into hibernation. This meant that spring would come early. By 1887, the local newspaper promoted the groundhog as the official weather forecaster. Based on today's records, scientists say that the groundhog is only 36 percent accurate in predicting weather.

_____

_____

_____

_____

_____

_____

_____

This week I learned:

- how to write a claim for argument-based paragraphs
- how to identify missing commas

NAME: _____ **DATE:** _____

Directions: Read the paragraph. Then, brainstorm at least three ideas to support each side of the chart below.

Long ago, farming cultures lived and slept by the rising and setting of the sun. But during the Industrial Revolution, adjustments were needed for workers to work more hours. Many countries began instituting daylight saving time as a way to get that extra hour in the afternoon. More work meant a better economy. Also, people were exposed to more sunlight, which meant a rise in vitamin D in their systems and time for more exercise outdoors. However, some say that daylight saving time contributes to more gasoline usage and pollution because people are out and about during the extra hour of sunlight. Experts disagree on whether or not we really need daylight saving time.

We Should Continue to Have Daylight Saving Time	We Should Do Away with Daylight Saving Time

NAME: _____ **DATE:** _____

Drafting
Daylight Saving Time

Directions: Do you think daylight saving time is necessary? Provide details to support your argument. Use the information in the chart on page 99 to help you draft your argument paragraph.

_____

_____

_____

_____

_____

_____

_____

_____

_____

_____

_____

_____

_____

_____

_____

_____

_____

Remember!

A strong argument paragraph includes:

- an introductory sentence stating your claim

- details that support your claim

- a concluding sentence that restates your claim

Cursive Practice *abc*

Directions: Use cursive to write one sentence that summarizes why you do or not think daylight saving time is necessary.

_____

_____

NAME: _____ DATE: _____

Directions: Explain why the simple sentences can be combined into compound sentences.

1. Some people argue that daylight saving time promotes better health. People get vitamin D from the sunshine.

   _____

   _____

   _____

2. The Industrial Revolution created a need for more workers. They instituted daylight saving time to add an extra hour into the day.

   _____

   _____

   _____

3. Some say that daylight saving time promotes more pollution. More people drive their cars in the daylight than at nighttime.

   _____

   _____

   _____

Remember!

To change a simple sentence into a compound sentence, join two sentences together using a comma and a conjunction such as *and*, *because*, or *so*.

NAME: _____ **DATE:** _____

Directions: Decide if each claim below is well written. Use the $\mathcal{L}$ symbol to delete the unnecessary information from the claims that are not well written. If necessary, explain what is wrong with the claims on the lines.

1. I think that daylight saving time should be mandated for all states and territories because it would keep everyone on the same schedule no matter where they lived.

_____

_____

2. Daylight saving time should not be practiced today because it is not as important to conserving energy and does not add to people's work day as it once did long ago.

_____

_____

3. I feel that daylight saving time should not be used because it is not adhered to in all states, it causes confusion for travelers, and it does not add value to people's extracurricular activities.

_____

_____

4. Daylight saving time should be used because it has the potential to conserve energy and it allows for people to extend their extracurricular activities to improve their health.

_____

_____

NAME: _____ **DATE:** _____

Directions: Do you think daylight saving time is necessary? Provide details to support your argument.

_____

_____

_____

_____

_____

_____

_____

_____

_____

_____

_____

_____

_____

_____

_____

_____

_____

_____

_____

NAME: _____ DATE:_____

Prewriting
Superhero Origins

Directions: Place check marks in the circles with ideas that should be included in an informative/explanatory paragraph about the origin of a superhero. Give reasons next to each circle you mark.

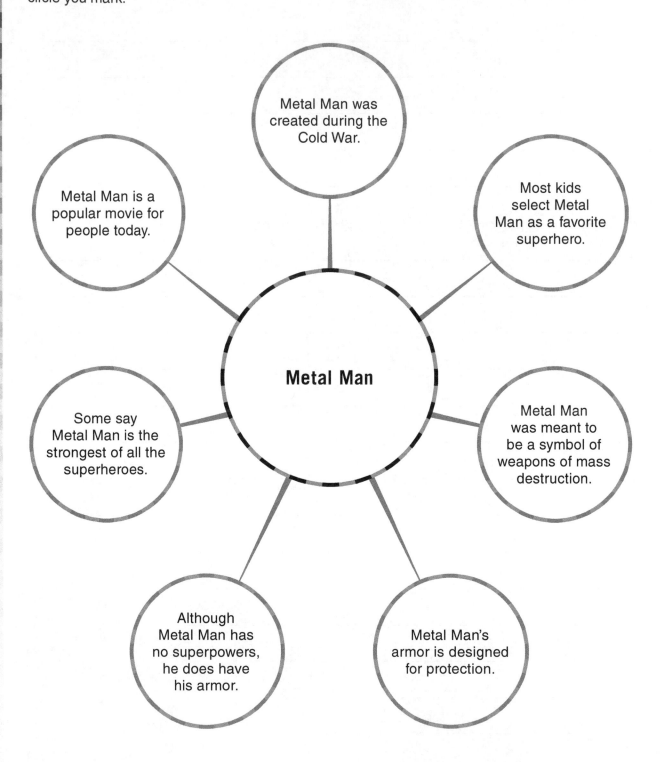

Metal Man was created during the Cold War.

Most kids select Metal Man as a favorite superhero.

Metal Man is a popular movie for people today.

Metal Man

Metal Man was meant to be a symbol of weapons of mass destruction.

Some say Metal Man is the strongest of all the superheroes.

Although Metal Man has no superpowers, he does have his armor.

Metal Man's armor is designed for protection.

NAME: _____ **DATE:** _____

Directions: Read the paragraph. Make notes in the margins about comparisons between the two superheroes. Draw arrows in the paragraph to show these comparisons.

Super Woman was created during World War II to fight the evil powers. Back then, people were afraid of their war enemies, so she gave people hope that she would defeat them. Later, she also fought other villains. She was a symbol for the new kind of woman who would rule the world. On the other hand, Wonderman came about during the Great Depression. Similarly, his purpose was to give power to people who felt they were powerless. At first, Wonderman fought common villains like powerful leaders, slumlords, and crooked politicians. These villains were the same ones that the common man had to fight back then.

Cursive Practice *abc*

Directions: Use cursive to write about the origin of your favorite superhero.

_____

_____

Revising

Superhero Origins

NAME: _____ **DATE:** _____

Directions: Read the sentences. Look for examples where two different words or phrases mean the same thing. Then, rewrite the sentences using only one of the words or phrases.

1. Since the 1960s, Super Woman became a symbol of feminism and women's rights as she fought her villains.

   _____

   _____

   _____

2. At first, Wonderman's foes and enemies included crooked politicians, unfair city government leaders, and slumlords that did not treat their tenants fairly.

   _____

   _____

   _____

3. Insect Man fans felt they could relate to him because he had been bullied and pushed around by others in his school before gaining the superpowers.

   _____

   _____

   _____

4. World War II was a difficult time for many Americans, so Mr. America gave them hope and promise that the war would be won through perseverance.

   _____

   _____

   _____

Boost Your Learning! 🚀

Thoughtful writers avoid using words that mean the same thing. It is better to be concise than to be repetitive.

NAME: _____ **DATE:** _____

Directions: Read the paragraph comparing two different superheroes. Then, use signal words in the Signal Word Bank to write two sentences about the paragraph.

Signal Word Bank

different	difference	but also	similarly	in contrast
same as	as well as	as opposed to	on the other hand	not only

Fans love Insect Man because people feel they can relate to him. When bitten by a radioactive spider during a field trip, Insect Man gained amazing strength and powers. He used powers to protect those who could not protect themselves. Mr. America survived polio as a child, which left him very weak. He gained strength by taking a super soldier serum. Insect Man was created in the early 1960s when people were afraid of what radioactive materials and nuclear war could do to people. Mr. America was created in WWII as a symbol of hope, courage, and ultimate patriotism. People were afraid that the war would continue to drag on, so this superhero provided encouragement to persevere.

1. _____

_____

_____

2. _____

_____

_____

Boost Your Learning!

To compare and contrast means to explain how two or more things are alike and how they are different.

NAME: _____ **DATE:** _____

Directions: Reread the paragraph. Then, explain why this is or is not a strong published piece on the lines below.

Super Woman was created during World War II to fight the evil powers. Back then, people were afraid of their war enemies, so she gave people hope that she would defeat them. Later, she also fought other villains. She was a symbol for the new kind of woman who would rule the world. On the other hand, Wonderman came about during the Great Depression. Similarly, his purpose was to give power to people who felt they were powerless. At first, Wonderman fought common villains like powerful leaders, slumlords, and crooked politicians. These villains were the same ones that the common man had to fight back then.

_____
_____
_____
_____
_____
_____
_____
_____
_____
_____

This week I learned:

- how to use signal words when explaining information about two subjects
- how to be concise to avoid repetition

NAME: _____ **DATE:** _____

Directions: Read the information about superheroes. Write reasons why each one would or would not make a good choice for an informative/explanatory paragraph.

Super Woman—superhuman strength; flight; super-speed; super-stamina; super-agility; proficient in hand-to-hand combat; ability to communicate with the animal kingdom; has a potion that forces people to tell the truth; a pair of indestructible bracelets; a tiara that serves as a projectile

_____

_____

Superman—tremendous strength; indestructible body; sharp senses—can hear faint sounds, telescopic and microscopic vision, x-ray vision; possesses heat vision that can heat up objects; moves, thinks, and reacts at superhuman speed; flight; possesses a force field

_____

_____

Insect Man—can cling to surfaces; superhuman strength; agile and acrobatic; web-slinging allows him to move quickly; insect sense that gives him an early warning detection of danger

_____

_____

Mr. America—does not have superhuman abilities; serum gives him the maximum human potential in speed, strength, reflexes, endurance, durability, and agility; bench presses 1,100 pounds (499 kilograms), runs a mile in about a minute; immune to diseases; heals faster than normal people

_____

_____

Drafting

Superhero Powers

NAME: _____ **DATE:**_____

Directions: Explain how superpowers are beneficial to superheroes and everyday citizens. Use your notes from page 109 to help you draft your informative/explanatory paragraph.

_____

_____

_____

_____

_____

_____

_____

_____

_____

_____

_____

_____

_____

> **Remember!**
>
> To draft a strong informative/explanatory paragraph, you should:
>
> - have an introductory and a concluding sentence
>
> - include details that support the main idea

Cursive Practice *abc*

Directions: Use cursive to write a superpower that you would like to have if you were a superhero.

_____

_____

_____

NAME: _____ **DATE:** _____

Directions: Read the signal words and phrases. Create four sentences about superhero powers. Include signal words or phrases in each one.

Signal Words and Phrases

either/or	alike	similarly
in contrast	same as	as well as
instead of	as opposed to	not only/but also
different/difference	on the other hand	

1. _____

_____

2. _____

_____

3. _____

_____

4. _____

_____

Time to Improve!

Look back at the draft you wrote on page 110. Look for places where signal words or phrases can help make your writing more clear.

Editing
Superhero Powers

NAME: _____ **DATE:** _____

Directions: Read the sentences below and look for examples where two different words mean the same thing. Use the ℓ symbol to cross out the repeated information. Then, explain why it was deleted.

1. Super Woman's potion forces people to be honest and tell the truth.

   _____

   _____

   _____

2. Wonderman responds, thinks, and reacts at superhuman speed and also possesses sharp senses.

   _____

   _____

   _____

3. Since possessing the skill and ability of web slinging, Insect Man can cling to buildings as he makes his way quickly to save people.

   _____

   _____

   _____

Boost Your Learning!

Being too wordy might make readers lose interest. Think about each word you use in your writing and select the ones that make the most impact.

NAME: _____ **DATE:** _____

Publishing
Superhero Powers

Directions: Explain how superpowers are beneficial to superheroes and everyday citizens.

_____

_____

_____

_____

_____

_____

_____

_____

_____

_____

_____

_____

_____

_____

_____

_____

_____

NAME: _____ DATE:_____

Directions: Place check marks in the circles with ideas that should be included in an informative/explanatory paragraph about black holes.

Some people worry that a black hole will eat up Earth.

A black hole can be as small as an atom.

Gravity pulls light into the middles of black holes, so scientists cannot see black holes.

In the past, many blockbuster movies have been made about black holes.

Black Holes

Black holes are interesting features to study in a galaxy.

A tiny black hole has the mass of a mountain.

A supermassive black hole is larger than the mass of 1 million suns.

A very large black hole can have mass that is 20 times larger than the mass found in the sun.

NAME: _____ **DATE:**_____

Directions: Read the paragraph. There are many key vocabulary words that help explain black holes. Underline the key vocabulary words that you see.

Black holes are not empty spaces. Within a black hole, gravity is so strong that everything is pulled inside. For example, a black hole's gravity can squeeze a star that is 10 times more massive than the sun into a space that is the size of a modern day city. A tiny black hole has the mass of a mountain even though it is as small as an atom. A very large black hole can have mass that is 20 times larger than the mass found in the sun. A supermassive black hole is larger than the mass of 1 million suns.

Boost Your Learning!

In an informative/explanatory paragraph, it is important to use key vocabulary words. In the text above, the key vocabulary words are science related. The words aren't often used, but they help explain science topics.

Cursive Practice 𝒶𝒷𝒸

Directions: Use cursive to write a sentence explaining what a black hole is.

_____

_____

NAME: _____ **DATE:** _____

Revising
Black Holes

Directions: Read each topic sentence. Write a concluding sentence to go with each one.

1. Black holes are exciting to study.

   _____

   _____

2. While black holes may look empty, they actually contain more mass than we can even imagine.

   _____

   _____

3. Black holes are large and full of mass.

   _____

   _____

Boost Your Learning! 🚀

Strong paragraphs include concluding sentences that summarize the main ideas of the paragraphs. A concluding sentence uses the information from the topic sentence. It tells the reader that the paragraph is complete.

NAME: _____ **DATE:** _____

Directions: Look for nonrestrictive information in the sentences. Then, use the ∧ symbol to add commas where necessary.

1. A black hole as large as it seems can be as small as an atom.

2. A tiny black hole has the mass of a mountain a concept that seems amazing to many people.

3. A very large black hole a fact that can be inconceivable for most people can have mass that is 20 times larger than the mass found in the sun.

4. A supermassive black hole something only usually shown in movies is larger than the mass of 1 million suns.

5. Gravity pulls light into the middles of black holes so scientists cannot see black holes.

Remember!

Nonrestrictive information can be set off with commas. Removing the information does not change the meaning of the sentence.

NAME: _____ DATE: _____

Publishing
Black Holes

Directions: Revisit the paragraph. Make notes in the margins of how you could make this a better informative/explanatory paragraph. Then, rewrite the new and improved paragraph below.

Black holes are not empty spaces. Within a black hole, gravity is so strong that everything is pulled inside. For example, a black hole's gravity can squeeze a star that is 10 times more massive than the sun into a space that is the size of a modern day city. A tiny black hole has the mass of a mountain even though it is as small as an atom. A very large black hole can have mass that is 20 times larger than the mass found in the sun. A supermassive black hole is larger than the mass of 1 million suns.

_____

_____

_____

_____

_____

_____

_____

_____

This week I learned:

- to notice key vocabulary words
- how to write concluding sentences
- how to add commas to nonrestrictive information

    #51529—180 Days of Writing

NAME: _____ **DATE:** _____

Directions: Explain why each statement should or should not be included in an informative/explanatory paragraph about space travel.

Space Travel Topic	Should this be included in an informative/explanatory paragraph? Why or why not?
NASA is planning on taking humans to the moon again by the year 2020 in preparation for travel to Mars.	
At some point in the future, humans dream of traveling to Mars, but know they will be unable to return back to Earth.	
Many people think space travel is the most exciting type of travel.	
NASA plans on using the *Orion* capsule for human travel because it is safer than the shuttle used in past years.	
In movies, people travel from planet to planet in a matter of hours.	

Drafting
Space Travel

NAME: _____ **DATE:** _____

Directions: Explain some of the preparations NASA is making for future space travel. Use the information from page 119 to help you draft your informative/explanatory paragraph.

_____

_____

_____

_____

_____

_____

_____

_____

_____

_____

_____

_____

_____

_____

> **Remember!**
>
> To draft a strong informative/explanatory paragraph, you should:
>
> - have an introductory and a concluding sentence
>
> - include details that support the main idea

Cursive Practice *abc*

Directions: If you could travel anywhere in space, where would you go? Write your answer in cursive.

_____

_____

_____

NAME: _____ DATE: _____

Directions: Read each topic sentence. Write a concluding sentence to go with each one.

1. Space travel is exciting to study.

   _____

   _____

2. While it may seem impossible to live on the moon, scientists are already making plans for humans to do just that.

   _____

   _____

3. Space travel is something NASA is preparing for in our lifetime.

   _____

   _____

Remember!

Strong paragraphs include a concluding sentence that summarizes the main idea of the paragraph. A concluding sentence uses the information from the topic sentence. A concluding sentence tells the reader that the paragraph is complete.

Time to Improve!

Look at the draft you wrote on page 120. Reread your concluding sentence. Try to revise it to make it stronger.

NAME: _____ DATE: _____

Editing
Space Travel

Directions: Read the sentences and look for places where commas are needed to set off nonrestrictive information. Use the ∧ symbol to add commas to the sentences.

1. NASA is planning on taking humans to the moon again by the year 2020 in preparation for travel to Mars something only the adventurous would do.

2. Humans the brave ones anyway dream of traveling to Mars but know they will be unable to return back to Earth.

3. Some people think space travel that is travel outside of our atmosphere is the most exciting type of travel.

4. NASA plans on using the *Orion* capsule a new type of spaceship for human travel because it is safer than the shuttle used in past years.

5. In the movies, people travel from planet to planet in a matter of hours which is something completely fictional.

Remember!

Nonrestrictive information can be set off with commas. Removing the information does not change the meaning of the sentence.

NAME: _____ **DATE:** _____

Directions: Explain some of the preparations NASA is making for future space travel.

_____

_____

_____

_____

_____

_____

_____

_____

_____

_____

_____

_____

_____

_____

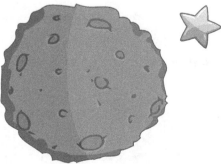

NAME: _____ DATE:_____

Directions: Read the planning notes and the short script for a play. Make notes about how well the script follows the planning notes in the margins of the script.

Planning Notes

Decide on at least two characters. (Cinderella and Prince)

Create a conflict. (Cinderella gets food poisoning while snacking at the ball.)

Plan a place to start or a beginning. (Cinderella becomes nauseated while having her first dance with Prince.)

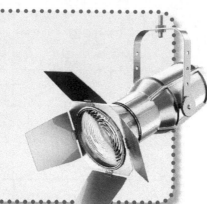

Prince: Are you feeling okay? Your hand feels clammy.

Cinderella: Oh, that. No, darling, I'm quite okay. It's just my nerves.

Prince: Your face is turning a light shade of green.

Cinderella: Do you know where the closest ladies' room is located? I think I need to take a short break.

Prince: But we just started dancing. I don't want to let you out of my sight. Was that your stomach rumbling?

Cinderella: I'm not used to eating so much food. I think I overdid it at the buffet.

Prince: Don't worry; I have a sickness bag that you can use. I use them when I go on long rides into the woods.

Cinderella: Thank goodness! I'm not sure I would make it to the ladies' room in time. Give me just a minute, and we can get back to dancing.

NAME: _____ **DATE:** _____

Directions: Use the context clues to explain what the underlined words mean.

Prince Charming: I always have a sickness bag for when my stomach gets upset. I use them when I go on long rides into the woods.

_____

_____

Cinderella: I frequently travel into the woods to get away from my dysfunctional family. I often wonder if there are any families who act normal.

_____

_____

Prince Charming: Perhaps if you loosen the corset around your waist your stomach might feel better. It is a shame that women have to wear these tight things.

_____

_____

Boost Your Learning! 🚀

In a narrative script, it is important to give challenging words context so the audience knows what the words mean.

Cursive Practice _abc_

Directions: Think of a title for the narrative script and write it in cursive.

_____

_____

NAME: _____ DATE:_____

Directions: Read the sentences and look for examples where two different words mean the same thing. Explain why some of the words should be taken out.

1. **Cinderella:** The very mention of the buffet makes me feel queasy and nauseated.

   _____

   _____

2. **Prince Charming:** Don't worry; I'll call a lady's maid or servant to help you.

   _____

   _____

3. **Cinderella:** Please hurry and act quickly. I don't think I can last much longer.

   _____

   _____

4. **Prince Charming:** They are on their way and should be here momentarily or shortly.

   _____

   _____

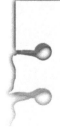

Boost Your Learning! 🚀

It is best to avoid using words that mean the same thing. Strong writers are concise and use only one word rather than being repetitive.

NAME: _____ **DATE:**_____

Directions: Read the sentences. Correct the capitalization errors using the ≡ symbol to show a word should be capitalized or the ╱ symbol to show a word should be lowercase.

1. The Classic story of cinderella is one that most people know.

2. One undeveloped character that we know very little about is prince Charming.

3. The Wicked Stepmother is a common character found in scripts.

4. Even with cinderella being the main character, the Audience really knows little about her.

5. Fairy godmother saves the day by giving Cinderella a dress and a way to the ball.

Remember!

Proper nouns should always be capitalized, while general nouns should always be lowercase.

NAME: _____ **DATE:** _____

Publishing

Live Theater Scripts

Directions: Revisit the script. Then, answer the questions.

Prince: Are you feeling okay? Your hand feels clammy.

Cinderella: Oh, that. No, darling, I'm quite okay. It's just my nerves.

Prince: Your face is turning a light shade of green.

Cinderella: Do you know where the closest ladies' room is located? I think I need to take a short break.

Prince: But we just started dancing our very first dance. I don't want to let you out of my sight. Was that your stomach rumbling?

Cinderella: I'm not used to eating so much food. I think I overdid it at the buffet.

Prince: Don't worry; I have a sickness bag that you can use. I use them when I go on long rides into the woods.

Cinderella: Thank goodness! I'm not sure I would make it to the ladies' room in time. Give me just a minute, and we can get back to dancing.

1. What makes this narrative script fun to read?

_____

_____

2. How could the author improve it?

_____

_____

This week I learned:

- how to use and understand context clues
- how to avoid using words that mean the same thing
- how to edit for capitalization

NAME: _____ DATE: _____

Prewriting

Television Show Scripts

Directions: Complete the chart with ideas to include in a television script. Think about how each section benefits a scripted narrative.

Decide on at least two characters. Describe what each character is like.

Create a conflict.

Plan a place to start or a beginning.

Show what happens in words and actions.

NAME: _____ **DATE:** _____

Drafting
Television Show Scripts

Directions: Draft a script for a scene in a new television show. Be sure to focus on one event and include multiple characters. Use your ideas from page 129 to help you draft your narrative script.

_____

_____

_____

_____

_____

_____

_____

_____

_____

_____

_____

_____

_____

_____

_____

> **Remember!**
>
> A strong narrative script:
>
> - includes characters
> - has a conflict
> - has a conclusion

Cursive Practice *abc*

Directions: Use cursive to write a title for your television show.

_____

NAME: _____ **DATE:** _____

Directions: Read the sentences. Look for examples where two different words mean the same thing. Explain why some information should be deleted.

1. **Detective:** The very mention of this criminal getting away makes me feel angry and mad.

   _____

   _____

2. **Mother:** Don't worry; I'll make sure the worker or laborer is around to feed the cat.

   _____

   _____

3. **Brother:** I'm feeling weak and frail. Please hurry up and call the doctor.

   _____

   _____

4. **Lawyer:** Everyone says that my job or profession is a noble one.

   _____

   _____

. . . .

Time to Improve!

Go back to your television script on page 130. Replace at least four words in the script with stronger or more interesting ones.

Editing

Television Show Scripts

NAME: _____ DATE:_____

Directions: Read the sentences. Use the ≡ or ╱ symbols to correct the capitalization errors.

1. Many shows on Television are Comedies, which are designed to make people laugh.

2. Television Scripts are similar to theater scripts in that they both tell the characters what to say.

3. It is important that Scripts tell the storyline in words and actions.

4. writers of Scripts should strive to use the strongest words that describe something.

5. Cartoons are Television Shows that can be designed for both children and adults depending on the content.

NAME: _____ **DATE:** _____

Directions: Write a script for a scene in a new television show. Be sure to focus on one event and include multiple characters.

_____

_____

_____

_____

_____

_____

_____

_____

_____

_____

_____

_____

_____

_____

_____

_____

_____

_____

_____

NAME: _____ DATE:_____

Prewriting
Comic Strips

Directions: Read the planning notes for a comic strip. Then, answer the question.

Planning Notes

Decide on at least two characters. (a worker and his boss)

Create a conflict. (The worker wants a promotion, but his boss does not think he is ready.)

Plan a place to start or a beginning. (The boss tells his worker what he thinks.)

What this is intended to show. (If you work hard, you will succeed.)

In this frame, the boss will tell the worker that he is not ready to be promoted like the worker wants. The image should show the boss yelling at the worker. The worker should look sad and defeated.	In this frame, the worker will try to prove himself by turning in what he thinks is a well-written report. The boss will reject it. The image should show that the boss is unhappy. The boss should be giving the poorly-written report back to the worker.
In this frame, the worker will prove he deserves the promotion. The image should represent the worker doing something worthy of getting the promotion, such as presenting growth for the company.	In this frame, the worker will get his promotion. The image should show the boss shaking the worker's hand.

1. How do planning notes help when creating a comic strip?

_____

_____

NAME: _____ **DATE:** _____

Directions: Read the comic strip about a worker who thinks he deserves a promotion. Then, answer the question.

1. How does the comic strip portray the argument getting solved?

_____

_____

· ·

Cursive Practice *abc*

Directions: Create names for the characters in the comic strip. Use cursive to write them.

_____   _____

Revising
Comic Strips

NAME: _____ DATE:_____

Directions: Read the sentences. Underline examples of figurative language. Label each one using the information in the chart.

Figurative Terms	Definitions
hyperbole	exaggerating the truth
metaphor	compares two unlike things
simile	compares two unlike things using the words *like* or *as*
onomatopoeia	naming an action according to what it sounds like
alliteration	using several words that all have the same sound

1. Writing reports is rain on a cloudy day.

   _____

2. Radical reports read ridiculously, so read them carefully.

   _____

3. I once saw a desk that was as big as a house!

   _____

4. Thump! The boss threw a stack of reports on the worker's desk.

   _____

5. Being a boss is like being a king.

   _____

 **Boost Your Learning!** 🚀

Strong writers help readers better understand their writing by using figurative language. Figurative language helps form images in readers' minds.

NAME: _____ **DATE:** _____

Directions: Read the sentences. Some of the commas are used incorrectly. Use the ℘ symbol to delete commas to make the sentences correct.

1. Comic strips, and movie reviews are often opinion pieces found in newspapers.

2. Comic strips can contain both animals, and people.

3. Writers often find it easier to express opinions, and thoughts using comic strips because they poke fun at ideas and things.

4. Since most comic strips are made up of dialogue, it is not necessary to use quotation marks, and commas.

5. Animals such as cats, and dogs, often take on human characteristics in comic strips.

Boost Your Learning!

Commas are not necessary when you only list two things. When listing three or more things, use **series commas** to separate the words.

Example: You might find people places and things in comics.
                                    ∧   ∧
                                    ,   ,

NAME: _____ DATE:_____

Directions: Revisit the comic strip. Then, answer the questions.

1. What argument does the author portray in the comic strip?

   _____

   _____

   _____

2. Does the author make his argument clear, or could the author state it more clearly? Explain.

   _____

   _____

   _____

NAME: _____ DATE: _____

Directions: Read the statements about movie reviews. Write *T* if the statement is true and *F* is the statement is false. Then, give reasons for your answers on the lines.

_____ **1.** Movie reviews should be unbiased.

_____

_____

_____ **2.** Movie reviews give information about something.

_____

_____

_____ **3.** Movie reviews express opinions.

_____

_____

_____ **4.** Movie reviews are pieces of fiction writing.

_____

_____

_____ **5.** Movie reviews should be read within the context of the writer.

_____

_____

Drafting
Movie Reviews

NAME: _____ **DATE:** _____

Directions: Think about a movie you have seen. Draft a review for it. Be sure to state your opinion of the movie and provide evidence to support your opinion. Use the information from page 139 to help you draft your argument paragraph.

_____

_____

_____

_____

_____

_____

_____

_____

_____

_____

_____

_____

_____

_____

_____

> **Remember!**
>
> A strong argument paragraph should:
>
> - begin with an introductory sentence that states your claim
>
> - include details that support your claim
>
> - end with a concluding sentence

Cursive Practice *abc*

Directions: Use cursive to write a sentence explaining what a movie reviewer could say to persuade you to see a movie.

_____

_____

_____

Revising
Movie Reviews

NAME: _____ **DATE:** _____

Directions: Read the sentences. Underline examples of figurative language. Label each one using the information at the bottom of the page.

1. Movies are time outs in a busy world. They make us stop and smell the roses every once in a while.

   _____

2. Movies mostly make me mad, but only because I know they are not true stories.

   _____

3. I once saw a movie that was as long as a year!

   _____

4. Crash! The pot landed on the floor, and the actor jumped to his feet.

   _____

5. Seeing movies is like living dreams through other people.

   _____

Time to Improve!

Go back to the draft you wrote on page 140. Add in at least two different kinds of figurative language.

Remember!

A *hyperbole* is exaggerating the truth.

A *metaphor* compares two unlike things.

A *simile* compares two unlike things using the words *like* or *as*.

An *onomatopoeia* names an action according to what it sounds like.

Alliteration uses several words that all start with the same sound.

NAME: _____ DATE: _____

Editing

Movie Reviews

Directions: The sentences below contain incorrect punctuation. Correct the punctuation errors using the ✐ symbol.

1. Movie reviews have both summaries, and opinions of the movie being reviewed.

2. People often consult movie reviews, either online, or in print, when deciding to see a movie.

3. Responsible movie reviewers always give reasons for their opinions, and ideas they express in these reviews.

4. A helpful tip for writers is to use figurative language to make the movie reviews more interesting to readers, and audiences.

5. Movie reviews are somewhat similar to comic strips in that they both express opinions, and are found in newspapers.

Remember!

Commas are used when listing more than two items or when setting off nonrestrictive information in a sentence.

Time to Improve!

Revisit the movie review you wrote on page 140. Edit your text to make sure you used commas appropriately. If you find any comma errors, use the correct editing mark to delete them from your paragraph.

NAME: _____ **DATE:** _____

Directions: Think about a movie you have seen. Write a review for it. Be sure to state your opinion of the movie and provide evidence to support your opinion.

_____
_____
_____
_____
_____
_____
_____
_____
_____
_____
_____
_____
_____
_____
_____
_____
_____
_____
_____
_____
_____

NAME: _____ **DATE:** _____

Prewriting
Fantasy Creatures

Directions: Think about how narrative texts are different from informative/explanatory texts. Then, place check marks in the circles with ideas that describe only narrative texts.

can give facts about real creatures

can tell made-up stories about creatures

can have creatures that go on quests

can include novels about creatures

can include real or imagined creatures

can have tables of contents describing creatures

can include headings and captions that explain creatures

Narrative Texts

can have a glossary about creatures

can include picture books about creatures

can be short stories about creatures

can have diagrams to show the anatomy of creatures

can have beginnings, middles, and ends to stories that include creatures

can have settings where creatures interact with one another

 #51529—180 Days of Writing   © Shell Education

NAME: _____ DATE: _____

Directions: Read the paragraph. Find at least three places where more details are needed to make the story more exciting. Underline these areas and make notes in the margins of what you might add to the story.

The wizard hung his head in defeat. He had lost his magic. What would he do? Most importantly, how would he retrieve the magic lamp and return it to the city to make it whole again? The wizard knew he had to tell his followers the truth, but could they be trusted with this important and embarrassing information? All he did know was that the dragon could never find out!

Cursive Practice *abc*

Directions: Use cursive to write at least two sentences that tell how you would feel if you experienced losing your magic lamp like the wizard does.

_____

_____

_____

_____

NAME: _____ **DATE:** _____

Directions: What details could you add to the text below to make the wizard an ideal character for a novel? Write your revisions to this text on the lines below.

The wizard hung his head in defeat. He had lost his magic. What would he do? Most importantly, how would he retrieve the magic lamp and return it to the city to make it whole again? The wizard knew he had to tell his followers the truth, but could they be trusted with this important and embarrassing information? All he did know was that the dragon could never find out!

_____

_____

_____

_____

_____

_____

_____

_____

_____

_____

_____

Boost Your Learning!

Great fantasy characters do things we would never do in real life. They are complex with motives, dreams, fears, and loves. These characters may include both flawed heroes and villains.

NAME: _____ **DATE:** _____

Editing

Fantasy Creatures

Directions: Read the sentences. The underlined pronouns are incorrect. Use the ℒ symbol to delete them. Then, write the correct word above it.

1. If the dragon really wants to stop the wizard and his elves, <u>they</u> can burn the forest down with one breath of fire.

2. Most people believe that dragons are fierce, but what would happen in a story if <u>he or she</u> were afraid of fire?

3. When one goes on a serious quest, <u>you</u> has to be ready for hardship and encounters with terrible creatures.

4. The elves ran out of bows and had to revert to karate to protect <u>his or her</u> wizard.

5. When the wizard finally found the magic lamp, <u>they</u> had to be careful not to wake the sleeping bats guarding it.

Boost Your Learning!

Avoid inappropriate pronoun shifts. Inappropriate pronoun shifts happen when a sentence shifts between first person (*I, we*) to second person (*you*), or third person (*he, she, they*).

NAME: _____ DATE:_____

Publishing Fantasy Creatures

Directions: Read the paragraph. Based on what you learned this week, add details on the lines provided to make the story more exciting.

The wizard hung his head in defeat. He had lost his magic. _____

_____

_____. What would he do? Most

importantly, how would he retrieve the magic lamp and return it to the city to make it whole

again? _____

_____.

The wizard knew he had to tell his followers the truth, but could they be trusted with this

important and embarrassing information? _____

_____

_____. All he did know was that the dragon could never

find out!

This week I learned:

- how to distinguish narrative writing from informative/explanatory writing
- how to add details to make characters more exciting
- how to recognize and correct inappropriate pronoun shifts

NAME: _____ **DATE:** _____

Directions: Read the titles. Write reasons why each one would or would not make a good title for a narrative fantasy.

Titles	Reasons Why This Makes or Does Not Make a Good Title
The Purposeless Magic	
The Source of the Mask	
How to Write Best Selling Fantasy Novels	
Getting Your Fantasy Novel Published	
The Family Thorn	
Gift in the Castle	
Ember in the Glass	

NAME: _____ **DATE:** _____

Directions: Imagine that you are a wizard about to embark on a daring adventure. Describe the events of your journey, including what happens and whom you meet along the way. Use your notes from page 149 to help you draft your narrative paragraph.

_____

_____

_____

_____

_____

_____

_____

_____

_____

_____

_____

_____

_____

_____

Remember! 👆

A strong narrative paragraph tells a story with a beginning, a middle, and an end.

Cursive Practice *abc*

Directions: Use cursive to write at least two sentences summarizing your fantasy story.

_____

_____

_____

_____

NAME: _____ **DATE:** _____

Directions: Revise the ideas presented in the sentences by adding more details about the quest. Write your revisions on the lines below.

1. Elvin knew he would have to climb the tall mountain to reach his one true love.

_____

_____

_____

2. The dwarves feared the dragon, and that was the one they would need to defeat to claim their gold.

_____

_____

_____

3. The boy knew the spider was waiting in the forest that surrounded the castle.

_____

_____

_____

Boost Your Learning! 🚀

Let your characters tell you what should happen in a story. They have motivations and fears, so let that drive your story. Also, explain why the quest is so difficult to achieve.

NAME: _____ DATE: _____

Editing
Fantasy Quests

Directions: Read the paragraph. It is missing pronouns. Use the ∧ symbol to add the pronouns.

The dragon was exhausted as looked back at the burning forest. He had no breath left and therefore no fire or smoke when suddenly saw the wizard and his entourage hiding behind the last tree standing. How did escape my fury? he questioned. Then, ran for the mountain expecting to be burned in the process, but the dragon had nothing left to threaten them with except large body.

Time to Improve!

Revisit the fantasy story you wrote on page 150. Edit your text to make sure you used pronouns appropriately. If there are any inappropriate pronoun shifts, use editing marks to replace them with the correct pronouns.

Remember!

Inappropriate pronoun shifts happen when a sentence shifts between first person (*I, we*) to second person (*you*) or third person (*he, she, they*). Be sure not to include inappropriate pronoun shifts in your writing!

NAME: _____ **DATE:** _____

Directions: Imagine that you are a wizard about to embark on a daring adventure. Describe the events of your journey, including what happens and whom you meet along the way.

_____

_____

_____

_____

_____

_____

_____

_____

_____

_____

_____

_____

_____

_____

_____

_____

_____

_____

NAME: _____ **DATE:**_____

Directions: Place check marks in the circles with ideas that you would include in an argument paragraph about rights and equality.

Gaining the right to vote was a step forward in equal rights for women.

Studying equal rights is something that should be left up to lawmakers not the general public.

Because of the Civil Rights Movement, schools became desegregated and African Americans learned alongside white children.

Rights and Equality

Today, many believe that people should get equal pay for equal work, regardless if they are male or female.

The fight for equal rights is something that is still ongoing today.

Equal rights should be studied because people like learning about what happened long ago.

NAME: _____ **DATE:** _____

Drafting

Rights and Equality

Directions: Read the paragraph. What evidence does the author use to make an argument that people should have equal rights? Underline that information, and make notes in the margins about the underlined parts.

Some people think that equal rights were settled long ago. However, people around the world are still fighting for equal rights. For example, in some parts of the world girls are not allowed to attend school because they are female. This generally happens because of a few different reasons. First, when families have to pay for education, they send their sons. The daughters stay home to help their mothers run the family. Second, not educating girls is sometimes tied to their religious beliefs. In societies like these, girls are fighting for the right to an equal education. Studies show that without an education, they are living with an increased risk of dying young or living in poverty. Girls that do attend school and learn to write, read, and count may eventually have children of their own. They will educate their families, too. In doing so, they will raise the economy of the entire country.

Cursive Practice

Directions: Use cursive to write a sentence explaining why equal rights are important.

_____

_____

NAME: _____ **DATE:** _____

Directions: Decide whether or not each claim is well written. Then, edit the claims for accuracy where needed.

1. I think that equal rights should be studied because it is an interesting topic.

   _____

   _____

   _____

2. Some people say that equal rights is an important topic, while others disagree.

   _____

   _____

   _____

3. I think that daughters stay home to help their mothers because of unequal rights.

   _____

   _____

   _____

Remember!

A *claim* is a statement that is argued and supported. Begin with explaining the subject. Then, add what you think about it. Finally, give a few reasons for your viewpoint.

Example: An equal education for girls will benefit society because the mortality rate is decreased, entire families are educated, and the economy is boosted.

NAME: _____ **DATE:** _____

Directions: Underline the run-on sentences in the paragraph. Use the ∧ symbol to add commas and conjunctions to make the compound sentence correct.

Conjunction Bank

| for | nor | but | and | or | yet | so |

Some people think that equal rights were settled long ago people around the world are still fighting for equal rights. For example, in some parts of the world girls are not allowed to attend school because they are female. This generally happens because of a few different reasons. First, when families have to pay for education, they send their sons the daughters stay home to help their mothers run the family. Second, not educating girls is sometimes tied to their religious beliefs. In societies like these, girls are fighting for the right to an equal education. Studies show that without an education, they are living with an increased risk of dying young or living in poverty. Girls that do attend school and learn to write, read, and count may eventually have children of their own they will educate their families, too. In doing so, they will raise the economy of the entire country.

Boost Your Learning! 🚀

To change a simple sentence into a compound sentence, join two sentences together using a comma and a conjunction. This helps to vary the length and structure of sentences within a paragraph. It also makes the paragraph more interesting for readers.

Publishing
Rights and Equality

NAME: _____   DATE:_____

Directions: Revisit the paragraph. On the lines below, write suggestions to the author for how she could improve it.

Some people think that equal rights were settled long ago. However, people around the world are still fighting for equal rights. For example, in some parts of the world girls are not allowed to attend school because they are female. This generally happens because of a few different reasons. First, when families have to pay for an education, they send their sons. The daughters stay home to help their mothers run the family. Second, not educating girls is sometimes tied to their religious beliefs. In societies like these, girls are fighting for the right to an equal education. Studies show that without an education, they are living with an increased risk of dying young or living in poverty. Girls that do attend school to learn to write, read, and count may eventually have children of their own. They will educate their families, too. In doing so, they will raise the economy of the entire country.

_____

_____

_____

_____

_____

_____

_____

_____

This week I learned:

- how to vary sentences by changing simple sentences into compound sentences

- how to write a claim for an argument paragraph

#51529—180 Days of Writing

NAME: _____ **DATE:** _____

Directions: How does diversity benefit the classroom? Use the outline to write notes and ideas to support your argument.

Begin with the subject: _____

_____

Add what you think about it: _____

_____

Give reasons for your viewpoint: _____

_____

_____

Write your claim here: _____

_____

_____

_____

NAME: _____ **DATE:** _____

Drafting Diversity

Directions: Do you think diversity is important in a classroom? Draft your argument, and include details to support your argument. Use your notes from page 159 to help you draft your paragraph.

_____

_____

_____

_____

_____

_____

_____

_____

_____

_____

_____

_____

_____

_____

_____

_____

Remember! 🕊️

A strong argument paragraph includes:

- an introductory sentence stating your claim

- details that support your claim

- a concluding sentence that restates your claim

Cursive Practice *abc*

Directions: Use cursive to write an introductory sentence to a paragraph about the argument you outlined.

_____

_____

_____

NAME: _____ **DATE:** _____

Directions: Revise each claim to make it stronger.

1. I think that diversity is a good thing because it offers people different points of views.

   _____

   _____

   _____

2. It is beneficial to have a diverse society.

   _____

   _____

   _____

3. I feel that diversity helps to educate and broaden people's minds.

   _____

   _____

   _____

Boost Your Learning! 🚀

Having a well-written claim is important to making your case.
Remember to be concise and clear in what you want to say.
Avoid using phrases such as *I think* and *I feel*.

Revising
Diversity

NAME: _____ **DATE:**_____

Directions: Use the ∧ symbol to add the missing conjunctions in the compound sentences.

1. People form opinions based on their backgrounds and experiences, what happened to them at some point in their lives affects how they view the world.

2. Other workers who are doing the same job are being paid more money because of their skin colors, this experience will most likely affect how this person feels about the topic of equal pay.

3. This experience will most likely affect how this person feels about the topic of equal pay, other people, who have never had this experience, can learn from this person's experience.

. . . .

Time to Improve!

Look back at your draft on page 160. Look for compound sentences, and make sure they use commas and conjunctions correctly.

Boost Your Learning!

Be careful not to use too many compound sentences. Sometimes using a simple sentence can make a strong statement and vary the sentence structure making the paragraph more interesting for readers.

NAME: _____ **DATE:** _____

Directions: Do you think diversity is important in a classroom? Write your argument, and include details to support your argument.

_____

_____

_____

_____

_____

_____

_____

_____

_____

_____

_____

_____

_____

_____

_____

_____

_____

_____

_____

_____

_____

NAME: _____ **DATE:** _____

Directions: Place check marks in the circles with ideas that might be found in an informative/explanatory paragraph about the sport of lacrosse.

The object of the game is to advance the ball into the goal guarded by the goalie.

Lacrosse is my favorite field sport on two feet.

American Indians, the first to play lacrosse, played to settle disputes, for spiritual reasons, to heal illnesses, and as a preparation for war.

Informative/Explanatory Writing

There are different rules for men's and women's lacrosse, with men's lacrosse being more physical.

To play the game, players use lacrosse sticks and other protective gear such as goggles and helmets.

About 300 years ago the Iroquois first introduced lacrosse to Europeans.

Many people think lacrosse is a fun sport to play.

NAME: _____ DATE:_____

Drafting

Lacrosse

Directions: Read the paragraph. Circle the main topics, and underline the supporting facts and examples.

Have you ever thought of playing a game that combines the rules from several different sports? Lacrosse, one of the fastest growing sports today, is a sport that combines many rules from basketball, hockey, and soccer. American Indians, the first to play lacrosse, played to settle disputes, for spiritual reasons, to heal illnesses, and as a preparation for war. About 300 years ago, the Iroquois first introduced lacrosse to Europeans. It is played on a field with sticks that have baskets for holding the ball and other protective gear such as pads, helmets, and goggles. Players take their positions on the field and the ball is tossed up. The object of the game is to advance the ball into the goal, which is guarded by the goalie. The ball advances down the field when players throw and catch it using their sticks. There are different rules for men's and women's lacrosse, with men's lacrosse being more physical.

Cursive Practice *abc*

Directions: Use cursive to write the main idea of the paragraph.

_____

_____

_____

_____

Revising Lacrosse

NAME: _____ DATE: _____

Directions: Revise each introductory sentence to make it more appealing to readers.

1. Lacrosse is a sport played by boys and girls today.

   _____

   _____

2. This paragraph will talk about lacrosse, a sport that combines rules from basketball, soccer, and hockey.

   _____

   _____

3. Lacrosse is a sport that is fun to play.

   _____

   _____

4. The rules of lacrosse make the game interesting.

   _____

   _____

5. Lacrosse is a sport that was first played by American Indians.

   _____

   _____

Boost Your Learning!

A strong introduction to a paragraph gets a reader interested in learning more about the topic. You want to grab the attention of the reader, so make the introductory sentence interesting!

NAME: _____ **DATE:** _____

Directions: Use the ∧ symbol to add commas to set apart the nonrestrictive information in each sentence.

1. The game of lacrosse the fastest growing sport in the United States is played with sticks and a ball.

2. Players advance the ball which is small and hard down the field by throwing it and running with it.

3. American Indians the first to play lacrosse played to settle disputes, for spiritual reasons, to heal illnesses, and as a preparation for war.

4. There are different rules for men's and women's lacrosse with men's lacrosse using more contact.

5. The object of the game is to advance the ball into the goal which is guarded by the goalie.

Remember!

Commas can be added to set apart nonrestrictive information in a sentence.

NAME: _____ DATE: _____

Publishing Lacrosse

Directions: Revisit the paragraph. Then, answer the questions.

Have you ever thought of playing a game that combines the rules from several different sports? Lacrosse, one of the fastest growing sports today, is a sport that combines many rules from basketball, hockey, and soccer. American Indians, the first to play lacrosse, played to settle disputes, for spiritual reasons, to heal illnesses, and as a preparation for war. About 300 years ago, the Iroquois first introduced lacrosse to Europeans. It is played on a field with sticks that have baskets for holding the ball and other protective gear such as pads, helmets, and goggles. Players take their positions on the field and the ball is tossed up. The object of the game is to advance the ball into the goal, which is guarded by the goalie. The ball advances down the field when players throw and catch it using their sticks. There are different rules for men's and women's lacrosse, with men's lacrosse being more physical.

1. Name two strengths of the paragraph.

   _____

   _____

   _____

2. What advice would you give the author to improve the paragraph?

   _____

   _____

   _____

This week I learned:

- how to write appealing introductory sentences
- how to develop a topic with supporting facts and examples
- how to use parentheses to set apart nonrestrictive information

NAME: _____ **DATE:** _____

Directions: Read the rugby rules. Then, write what is unusual or interesting about this sport next to each rule.

Rugby Rules	What I Notice
The game of rugby is called a *match*.	
The team with the most points after 80 minutes wins.	
The ball can advance down the field by running it or kicking it but not throwing it forward.	
Players tackle the opposing players to the ground to gain control of the ball.	
To score, the ball needs to land in the goal on the opposite end of the field.	
A *try* is when a player crosses the goal line and places the ball on the ground with a hand on it. A *goal* happens when the player kicks the ball in between the goal posts and above the crossbar.	

NAME: _____ DATE: _____

Drafting

Rugby

Directions: Explain how the game of rugby is played. Include details to make it easy to understand. Use the rugby rules from page 169 to help you draft your informative/explanatory paragraph.

_____

_____

_____

_____

_____

_____

_____

_____

_____

_____

_____

> ### Remember!
>
> A strong informative/explanatory paragraph includes:
>
> - an introductory and a concluding sentence
> - details that support the main idea
> - complete sentences

Cursive Practice *abc*

Directions: Use cursive to write two new rules you might add to the game of rugby.

_____

_____

_____

_____

_____

_____

NAME: _____ DATE:_____

Revising
Rugby

Directions: Explain why the sentences are or are not strong introductions.

1. Have you ever thought about playing rugby?

   _____

   _____

2. This paragraph will talk about rugby, a sport that is similar to football and soccer.

   _____

   _____

3. Rugby is an interesting and fun sport to play.

   _____

   _____

4. If you have ever wanted to play an aggressive sport, rugby might be the sport for you!

   _____

   _____

· ·

Time to Improve!

Go back to the informative/explanatory piece you wrote about rugby. Revise your introductory sentence to make sure that it grabs the attention of the reader.

NAME: _____ **DATE:** _____

Editing · Rugby

Directions: Use the ∧ symbol to add commas to set apart the nonrestrictive information in each sentence.

1. The game of rugby one of the most aggressive sports today is played on a field that is 328 feet (100 meters) long.

2. Players advance the ball down the field by kicking it and running with it but not throwing it forward.

3. A *try* one way to score a point is when a player takes the ball to the goal and places it on the ground with a hand on top of the ball.

4. A *goal* another way to score a point is when the player kicks the ball inside the goal and above the crossbar.

5. The object of the game which is a difficult one to do is to score more points than your opponent within an 80-minute time frame.

Time to Improve!

Go back to the piece you wrote on page 170 about rugby. Edit your text to set off nonrestrictive information with commas. If you did not use nonrestrictive information, find places to add some to your paragraph.

Remember!

Nonrestrictive information is information that would not change the meaning of the sentence if it were deleted.

NAME: _____ **DATE:** _____

Directions: Explain how the game of rugby is played. Include details to make it easy to understand.

_____

_____

_____

_____

_____

_____

_____

_____

_____

_____

_____

_____

_____

_____

_____

_____

_____

NAME: _____ DATE: _____

Prewriting

Domestic Pets

Directions: Place check marks in the circles with ideas that could be used in an informative/ explanatory paragraph about pets.

Charlotte's Web is a story about a girl who treated a pig on the farm as her pet.

Some families are unable to have certain pets because of allergies.

Every family should have a pet.

Pets such as cats need attention, love, food, and shelter.

For some, fish make the ultimate pet because they are less demanding.

To raise a dog, a family must be willing to feed and take care of the dog's needs.

Pets

Once upon a time there was a pet named Curious George.

Potbelly pigs are the most ideal pets because they do not shed or bark.

Some people adopt pets from shelters or rescue groups while others get their pets from breeders.

NAME: _____ **DATE:** _____

Directions: Identify whether the sentences in the paragraph are declarative (*D*), exclamatory (*E*), imperative (*IM*), or interrogative (*IN*).

_____Have you ever thought of the benefits of owning a pet? _____Studies show that pets can improve the health and well-being of people. _____For example, research shows that children who live in homes with cats and dogs have fewer chances of developing allergies. _____They also have higher immune systems as they grow older. _____Pets have shown to reduce blood pressure in older adults. _____Pets can even reduce anxiety! _____So, before you take medicine for a health problem, think about getting a pet first.

Remember!

Declarative sentences state facts or arguments and end with periods.

Exclamatory sentences express strong emotions and end with exclamation points.

Imperative sentences give commands and can end with periods or exclamation points.

Interrogative sentences ask questions and end with question marks.

Cursive Practice *abc*

Directions: Use cursive to write a sentence explaining why owning pets is beneficial for people.

_____

_____

Revising
Domestic Pets

NAME: _____ **DATE:** _____

Directions: Each sentence below has nonrestrictive information that should be set off with commas. Add in the commas to each sentence to set off this information.

1. About 62 percent of families two out of every three in the United States own pets.

2. Some people such as older generations who live alone own pets because they want companionship.

3. While some people get their pets from breeders and stores, others go to shelters places where people can adopt pets to find the newest members of their households.

4. Owning pets something that two out of three families do has been proven to offer health benefits like lowered blood pressure.

Remember!

Commas can be used to add nonrestrictive information to a sentence.

NAME: _____ DATE:_____

Editing
Domestic Pets

Directions: The sentences contain incorrect punctuation. Correct the punctuation errors using the ℒ symbol to show that they do not belong in the sentence.

1. Many people enjoy pets, because pets do not judge them based on appearance, or social status.

2. Pets do not care whether people are beautiful, or ugly; they simply are loyal to their owners.

3. Since fish can have a calming effect on people, many doctors have large fish and small fish in their waiting rooms.

4. Because pets depend on their owners for food, and shelter, many parents use pets as a way of teaching their children responsibility.

5. Animals, such as dogs, and horses, can help their owners get more exercise, because most dogs require walks every day.

Remember!

Commas are not necessary when only listing two things. When listing three or more things, use commas to separate the words or phrases.

Publishing

Domestic Pets

NAME: _____ DATE:_____

Directions: Revisit the paragraph. On the lines, write suggestions for the author about how she can imporve it.

Have you ever thought of the benefits of owning a pet? Studies show that pets can improve the health and well-being of people. For example, research shows that children who live in homes with cats and dogs have fewer chances of developing allergies. They also have higher immune systems as they grow older. Pets have shown to reduce blood pressure in older adults. Pets can even reduce anxiety! So, before you take medicine for a health problem, think about getting a pet first.

_____

_____

_____

_____

_____

_____

This week I learned:

- to vary sentences by including interrogative, imperative, and exclamatory sentences

- to use commas to add nonrestrictive information to sentences

NAME: _____ **DATE:** _____

Directions: Read the facts about exotic pets. Then, explain why each one may or may not be the ideal pet for you.

Exotic Pets	Ideal or Not Ideal Pet?
Flying Squirrel nocturnal animal bonds easily with owner loves sleeping in pouches uses a gliding membrane to fly in a downward direction needs room to run and jump diet of nuts, seeds, mealworms, moths	
Bearded Dragon easy to tame very social and likes to hang out on owner's shoulders grows to about two feet (61 centimeters) has strict feeding habits needs an environment with the right humidity, warmth, coolness, and UV light can live 10–20 years needs a 55 gallon (208 liter) tank	
Tarantula needs little space can live 30 years too much handling can cause it stress venomous bite but is comparable to a wasp sting can release tiny hairs that can irritate human skin not social with other animals	

Drafting
Exotic Pets

NAME: _____ **DATE:** _____

Directions: Choose an exotic pet. Then, draft a paragraph explaining the characteristics of that animal. Use your notes from page 179 to help you draft your informative/explanatory paragraph.

_____

_____

_____

_____

_____

_____

_____

_____

_____

_____

_____

_____

_____

_____

_____

_____

> **Remember!**
>
> A strong informative/explanatory paragraph includes:
>
> - an introductory and a concluding sentence
>
> - details that support the main idea
>
> - complete sentences

Cursive Practice *abc*

Directions: Use cursive to write why an exotic animal makes a good pet.

_____

_____

_____

#51529—180 Days of Writing   © Shell Education

NAME: _____ **DATE:** _____

Directions: Read the sentences. Label each sentence as *R* for restrictive or *N* for nonrestrictive. Then, create two of your own sentences. Have one sentence include restrictive information and the other sentence include nonrestrictive information.

_____ 1. Even though tarantulas have venomous bites, something comparable to a wasp sting, many people still choose to own them as pets.

_____ 2. The bearded dragon, which is very social and likes to hang out on its owners' shoulders, can live anywhere from 10 to 20 years.

_____ 3. The flying squirrel, originally a nocturnal animal, can adapt to being awake during the day to socialize with its owners.

4. _____

_____

_____

5. _____

_____

_____

Time to Improve!

Go back to the paragraph you wrote about owning an exotic pet on page 180. Revise at least two sentences to include commas and nonrestrictive information.

NAME: _____ DATE: _____

Editing
Exotic Pets

Directions: The sentences contain incorrect punctuation. Use the ✐ symbol to correct the punctuation errors.

1. A flying squirrel uses a gliding membrane to fly in a downward direction, and needs room to run and jump.

2. Bearded dragons need environments with just the right temperatures, and UV lights.

3. For someone wanting a pet to live a long time, tarantulas can be the ideal pet because they can live up to 20 years?

4. Owners of tarantulas should avoid touching them too often, because too much handling can cause the tarantula to be stressed:

5. Exotic pets are not for everyone; but they can make great pets for some people who are willing to make accommodations.

Time to Improve!

Look back at the draft you wrote on page 180. Edit your text to make sure you used punctuation marks appropriately. Use editing marks to make any necessary corrections.

NAME: _____ **DATE:** _____

Directions: Choose an exotic pet. Then, write a paragraph explaining the characteristics of that animal.

_____

_____

_____

_____

_____

_____

_____

_____

_____

_____

_____

_____

_____

_____

_____

_____

NAME: _____ DATE:_____

Prewriting — Eating

Directions: Explain whether or not each idea is appropriate for an argument paragraph.

1. I think we should eat healthy because it makes people feel better.

_____

_____

2. We should eat healthy because good nutrients affect our brains, movement, and bodies.

_____

_____

Should We Care About What We Eat?

3. I feel that eating healthy is good for us, so most people should eat healthy.

_____

_____

4. We should eat healthy because research has proven the benefits of eating nutritious meals.

_____

_____

NAME: _____ DATE: _____

Directions: Read the paragraph. What evidence does the author use to make a claim that eating healthy is important for our bodies? Underline that information, and make notes in the margins about the underlined parts.

Some people might doubt the importance of eating healthy. But the latest research seems to prove that good nutrients affect our brains, movement, and bodies. For example, too much sugar interferes with our ability to concentrate. We get distracted easily and tire out more if we consume too much sugar. But sugar definitely makes things taste yummy. If we eat more fruits and vegetables, our blood pressure may be lower. Every now and then, it might be okay to enjoy a cupcake. But it's best to stick to a nutritious diet if we want our brains and bodies to stay healthy.

Cursive Practice

Directions: Use cursive to write one more reason why eating healthy is good for our bodies.

_____

_____

NAME: _____ **DATE:** _____

Revising
Eating

Directions: Decide whether or not the claims are well written. Then, revise the sentences to make them better.

1. I think that eating healthy should be important to us because it helps our brains, movement, and bodies.

_____

_____

_____

2. Some people say that eating healthy should be a priority in our homes, and others disagree, saying that the public is making too big a fuss about it.

_____

_____

_____

3. Eating healthy is important because it improves our brain function, movement ability, and the overall health of our bodies.

_____

_____

_____

4. I feel that eating healthy is a good thing to do because it makes us feel better.

_____

_____

_____

Remember!

A claim is a statement that is argued and supported in writing. Begin with the subject. Then, add what you think about it. Finally, give a few reasons for your viewpoint.

NAME: _____ DATE:_____

Directions: Revise the two underlined sentences into compound sentences. Use the ∧ symbol to insert a comma before each conjunction. Then, rewrite the sentences on the lines below.

Some people might doubt the importance of eating healthy. But the latest research seems to prove that good nutrients affect our brains, movement, and bodies. For example, too much sugar interferes with our ability to concentrate. We get distracted easily and tire out more if we consume too much sugar. But sugar definitely makes things taste yummy. Studies show that if we eat more fruits and vegetables, our blood pressure may be lower. Every now and then, it might be okay to enjoy a cupcake. But it's best to stick to a nutritious diet if we want our brains and bodies to stay healthy.

1. _____

_____

_____

2. _____

_____

_____

Remember!

To change a simple sentence into a compound sentence, join two sentences together using a comma and a conjunction. This helps to vary the length and structure of sentences within a paragraph. It also makes the paragraph more interesting for readers.

NAME: _____ **DATE:** _____

Directions: Revisit the paragraph. Then, answer the questions.

Some people might doubt the importance of eating healthy diets. But the latest research seems to prove that good nutrients affect our brains, movement, and bodies. For example, too much sugar interferes with our ability to concentrate. We get distracted easily and tire out more if we consume too much sugar. But sugar definitely makes things taste yummy. If we eat more fruits and vegetables, our blood pressure may be lower. Every now and then, it might be okay to enjoy a cupcake. But it's best to stick to a nutritious diet if we want our brains and body to stay healthy.

1. What argument is the author trying to make? How do you know?

_____

_____

_____

_____

2. List two examples of ways the author supports his argument.

_____

_____

_____

_____

This week I learned:

- how to vary sentences by changing simple sentences into compound sentences

- how to write a claim for an argument-based paragraph

NAME: _____ **DATE:** _____

Directions: Review the information in the paragraph about how exercise benefits students. Then, write a claim that explains your opinion using the following outline.

Doctors and researchers recommend that students strive to get exercise every day. Studies show that students who exercise regularly have stronger muscles and bones. Students who exercise regularly tend to sleep better at night, too. They also can handle emotional challenges better than their peers who do not exercise. In fact, a recent study showed that students who exercise do better on creativity tests than those who do not regularly exercise. Some form of exercise each day will help students to perform their very best both in and outside of school.

Begin with the subject: _____

_____

Add what you think about it: _____

_____

Give reasons for your viewpoint: _____

_____

_____

Write your claim here: _____

_____

_____

_____

Drafting
Exercising

NAME: _____ **DATE:** _____

Directions: Some people think exercising is a good thing, while others think it is not a good thing. Explain which side you support and why. Use the information from page 189 to help you draft your argument paragraph.

_____

_____

_____

_____

_____

_____

_____

_____

_____

_____

_____

_____

Remember!

A strong argument paragraph includes:

- an introductory sentence stating your claim

- details that support your claim

- a concluding sentence that restates your claim

Cursive Practice *abc*

Directions: Use cursive to write a sentence about your favorite way to exercise.

_____

_____

_____

NAME: _____ **DATE:** _____

Directions: Change the simple sentences into compound sentences. Make sure to add commas and conjunctions.

1. Studies show that students who exercise are better problem solvers. If you want to think more creatively, you need to exercise.

   _____

   _____

   _____

2. Exercising helps students develop stronger bones. Students should strive to get more exercise every day.

   _____

   _____

   _____

3. Doctors worry about students' health. More and more students spend time inside playing video games instead of playing sports outdoors.

   _____

   _____

   _____

. . . .

Time to Improve!

Go back to the paragraph you wrote on page 190 about how exercise can benefit students. Revise your paragraph to include both simple and compound sentences.

NAME: _____ **DATE:** _____

Editing
Exercising

Directions: Correct the punctuation errors using the ℒ symbol. Then, decide if each claim below is a well-written claim or not.

1. I think that exercise helps students, because studies show it promotes better sleeping at night, and thinking during the day.

_____

_____

_____

2. Exercise is important because it builds students' problem-solving skills, and creative thinking skills.

_____

_____

_____

3. I feel that exercise is important because it promotes better bone, and muscle growth in students.

_____

_____

_____

4. Students should strive to get more exercise, because studies show there are great benefits, to their bodies, minds, and habits.

_____

_____

_____

NAME: _____ **DATE:** _____

Directions: Some people think exercising is a good thing, while others think it is not a good thing. Explain which side you support and why.

_____

_____

_____

_____

_____

_____

_____

_____

_____

_____

_____

_____

_____

_____

_____

_____

_____

_____

_____

_____

_____

ANSWER KEY

The activity pages that do not have specific answers to them are not included in this answer key. Students' answers will vary on these activity pages, so check that students are staying on task.

Week 1: Places I've Been

Day 1 (page 14)

Checked circles:

can tell stories about going on cruises

can have characters that go to the mountains

can include real or imagined travel to new places

can have sequences of events that tell about adventures

can include novels about sailing on oceans

can be short stories about going to Grandma's house

can have beginnings, middles, and ends to adventures

can have settings to show where adventures take place

Day 2 (page 15)

Student answers will vary, but may include:

The first place we stopped for gas was the gas station.

That was bad news because all the snacks in our car were ruined when my little brother spilled his milk.

Then, the worst thing happened, but I won't talk about it now.

Day 3 (page 16)

The sentences should be in the following order: 1) When she pulled on the cord, the balloon began to rise far into the sky. 2) At first, the thin air took her breath away. 3) But then, her lungs grew accustomed to the altitude. 4) Farther and farther she flew until she couldn't see her village anymore. 5) Only then did it dawn on her that she might not be able to find her way back to the village.

Day 4 (page 17)

1. If a student really wants to have fun, <u>he or she</u> can go to the backyard for an afternoon adventure.
2. Most students enjoy flying on planes instead of driving to the mountains because it takes too long for <u>them</u> to reach their final destinations.
3. Whenever one spends time in the rainforest, <u>one</u> has to be ready for the rain showers at any moment.
4. The train zoomed past <u>them</u> so fast that their tickets blew from their hands.
5. When Emily went to the secret garden, <u>she</u> had to be careful of the poisonous flowers.

Week 2: Places I Want to Go

Day 1 (page 19)

Title	Reason
Adventures are Always Fun for Everyone	This is not a good title for a narrative because it is an argument-based title and would be better suited for argument writing.
The Day We Ended Up In Outer Space	This is a good title for a narrative because it prepares the reader to hear the story of what happens.
The Reasons Our Cruise Line is the Best	This is not a good title for a narrative because it is an argument-based title and would be better suited for argument writing.
How to Plan the Most Efficient Camping Trip for Your Family	This is not a good title for a narrative because it is a how-to title and would be better suited for informative/explanatory writing.
He Never Believed He Would See the Ocean	This is a good title for a narrative because it prepares the reader to hear the story of what happens.
The Story of the Rescue Boat Adventure	This is a good title for a narrative because it prepares the reader to hear the story of what happens.

Day 4 (page 22)

I/we, I/we, I/we, my/our, my/our, I/we, I/we, I/we, me/us, me, I/we

Day 5 (page 23)

See Narrative Writing Rubric on page 208.

ANSWER KEY *(cont.)*

Week 3: Gods and Heroes

Day 1 (page 24)

Checked circles:

Odysseus and his men encountered the Cyclops, the one-eyed son of the god Poseidon

The Greeks used myths for entertainment.

Zeus is the god of the sky in Greek mythology.

The Trojan horse myth is a story about how the Greek army hid inside a large wooden horse.

Day 2 (page 25)

Main topic: Mythology explained the religious beliefs of the ancient Greeks.

Supporting examples: The Greeks worshiped the gods, including Zeus (the god of the sky), Poseidon (the god of the sea), and Hades (the god of the underworld). The gods spoke to the Greeks through oracles, or priests, who told them about the future.

Main topic: The Greeks also used myths to explain the things they did not understand about their world.

Supporting examples: For example, Pandora's box explains how evil came into the world. Heroes emerged from many of these stories.

Main topic: The Greeks used myths for entertainment and performed plays about these myths in amphitheaters.

Supporting examples: One example is the journey of Odysseus from Troy to his home. In this story, he encounters a Cyclops and the Land of the Dead. But after years of trials, this hero makes it home to his wife and kingdom.

Day 4 (page 27)

1. The Greeks worshipped gods, including Zeus, god of the sky.
2. The story of Odysseus, a Greek hero who finds his way home, is a very old tale.
3. Zeus, the god of the sky and king of Mount Olympus, is symbolized by a thunderbolt and an eagle.
4. Persephone was kidnapped by Hades, also known as the god of the underworld.
5. You can identify the statues of Poseidon, the god of the sea, because he is often shown with a trident.

Week 4: Nature of the World

Day 4 (page 32)

1. According to Greek myths, seasons came to be when Persephone was dragged away to the underworld by Hades, the god of the dead.
2. Zeus, the god of the sky, orders the Cyclopes to hammer lightning bolts, which cause earthquakes to happen.
3. Sailors rely on Poseidon, the god of the sea, for safe travels and smooth voyages.

Day 5 (page 33)

See Informative/Explanatory Writing Rubric on page 207.

Week 5: Fairy Tales: For Children or Adults?

Day 1 (page 34)

Answers will vary, but each should include an idea that the content is violent and is not appropriate for children.

Day 2 (page 35)

Claim: Fairy tales are filled with bias.

Evidence: In the original story, it is the mother who wants to kill Snow White. It is changed to her stepmother, which shows bias against stepmothers.

Claim: Fairy tales are filled with violence.

Evidence: Snow White's biological mother wants to kill her. The stepmother is made to wear shoes made from iron and dance until she dies. The stepmother falls from a cliff and dies.

Day 3 (page 36)

1. The sentence means that the story is 200 years old, and it still frightens children. (nonrestrictive)
2. The sentence means that the apple is 200 years old, and that the old apple frightens children. (restrictive)
3. The sentence means that the stories are old but can be bought in bookstores today. (nonrestrictive)
4. The sentence says that the actual old stories from the early 1800s can be bought today in bookstores. (restrictive)

Day 4 (page 37)

pronoun: she; **antecedent:** evil queen

pronoun: them; **antecedent:** Hansel and Gretel

pronoun: her; **antecedent:** Cinderella

pronoun: they; **antecedent:** the Three Little Pigs

Day 5 (page 38)

1. The author feels that all fairy tales are better suited for adults.

ANSWER KEY (cont.)

Week 6: Fairy Tales: A Villain's Perspective

Day 3 (page 41)

1. The story of the Frog Prince, which originally showed a very selfish and bratty princess, said that they lived happily ever after. (The sentence seemed to say that the frog prince showed a selfish and bratty princess.)
2. The tale of the evil queen giving Snow White a poisoned apple, which is almost 200 years old, might be different if told from the queen's perspective. (The sentence seemed to say that the poisoned apple was 200 years old.)
3. The Wolf, originally depicted as the villain in the story, paints a picture that makes the Three Little Pigs look like the true villains in the story. (The sentence seemed to say that the villain in the story paints a picture.)

Day 4 (page 42)

1. **pronoun:** he; **antecedent:** wolf
2. **pronoun:** she; **antecedent:** witch
3. **pronoun:** her; **antecedent:** stepmother
4. **pronoun:** her; **antecedent:** evil queen

Day 5 (page 43)

See Argument Writing Rubric on page 206.

Week 7: Unsolved Mysteries

Day 1 (page 44)

Answers will vary, but each should include reasons for why students think that Chet and Ginger committed the crime.

Day 3 (page 46)

1. his (This pronoun shows possession of the car.)
2. her (This pronoun shows possession of chocolate.)
3. her (This pronoun shows possession of knowledge of history.)
4. their (This pronoun shows possession of evidence.)

Day 4 (page 47)

1. *Wilamena's* is replaced with *Her*.
2. *Ginger's* is replaced with *Her*.
3. *Chet's* is replaced with *his*.
4. *Wilamena's* is replaced with *her*.
5. *Wilamena's* is replaced with *her*.

Week 8: Ghost Story or Not?

Day 1 (page 49)

Answers can vary but may include: Instead of sleepwalking, which used to be a problem for me, I began having nightmares. I woke suddenly and found that my hands and face were spattered with something sweet. Flour paw prints covered the floor. Then, I saw the cupcake on my table. It was the exact cupcake in my dream.

Day 3 (page 51)

my possesses *pet dog*
my possesses *birthday*
my possesses *birthday*
my possesses *room*
my possesses *favorite*
my possesses *day*
her possesses *spirit*
my possesses *hands and face*
my possesses *table*
my possesses *dream*

Day 4 (page 52)

1. Replace *Kara's* with *her*.
2. Replace *Rosebud's* with *her*.
3. Replace *Rosebud's* with *her*.
4. Replace *Kara's* with *her*.

Day 5 (page 53)

See Argument Writing Rubric on page 206.

Week 9: Living as Royalty

Day 3 (page 56)

1. (its) objective
2. (he) subjective
3. (him) objective
4. (he) subjective
5. They (subjective)

Day 4 (page 57)

1. He served the lord of the castle by fighting. (He is in the subjective case because it is the subject.)
2. At just seven years old, he had to wait tables and help the lord dress for the day. (He is in the subjective case because it is the subject.)
3. The castle served as a school for them. (Them is in the objective case because it is the object.)
4. After serving for seven years, they became knights and learned how to defend the lord. (They is in the subjective case because it is the subject.)

ANSWER KEY (cont.)

Week 10: Living as Peasants

Day 3 (page 61)
1. S; They
2. O; them
3. O; them
4. O; they
5. S; he

Day 5 (page 63)
See Narrative Writing Rubric on page 208.

Week 11: Renaissance Artists

Day 1 (page 64)
Checked circles:
Michaelangelo remembered the misery he felt painting the Sistine Chapel.

While painting *The Last Supper*, Leonardo da Vinci experimented with painting on dry plaster.

Rumor has it that Michaelangelo and Leonardo da Vinci were competitors and did not like one another.

Day 3 (page 66)
Student answers can vary but may include:

Leonardo da Vinci painted *The Last Supper* on the walls of a dining hall in a monastery. He did not paint on wet plaster. Instead, he painted directly on the wall, and the painting deteriorated quickly. The painting needed restoration. For years, people have tried to restore the painting until the last restoration in 1978. It took 20 years to complete.

Day 4 (page 67)
1. *Mona Lisa*, Leonardo da Vinci's most famous painting, is housed in the Louvre in Paris, France.
2. Michelangelo wrote a poem about his work in the Sistine Chapel, something that was very unpleasant for him.
3. Patrons hired artists, such as Leonardo da Vinci and Michelangelo, to paint and sculpt works of art.
4. The sculpture of David is out of proportion, something Michelangelo did on purpose, but still commands awe from viewers.

Week 12: Renaissance Inventions

Day 3 (page 71)
Student answers can vary but may include: Before the invention of the printing press, it could take months or years for monks to painstakingly copy each book by hand. It was a long process. Books were expensive to buy for the everyday man until Johannes Gutenberg came along. He invented the printing press. He took things that were already invented, such as ink, paper, moveable type, and a press and combined them. Suddenly, books were cheaper and quicker to reproduce.

Day 4 (page 72)
1. The flush toilet, invented by Sir John Harrington, was created for Queen Elizabeth in her castle.
2. Johannes Gutenberg combined ink, paper, moveable type, and a press to create the first printing press, something that has changed book making forever.
3. Galileo Galilei, a scientist during the Renaissance, used the telescope to study the heavens and wrote about his findings in his book, *Starry Messenger*.
4. The dome of the cathedral, a beautiful building in Italy, was engineered by the architect Filippo Brunelleschi.

Day 5 (page 73)
See Narrative Writing Rubric on page 208.

Week 13: Pirates and Treasures

Day 3 (page 76)
Student answers can vary but may include:
1. Perhaps the most famous three-year pirate in history was Blackbeard, but many knew him by his real name, Edward Teach.
2. Because he worked for Queen Elizabeth, Sir Francis Drake was nicknamed the Queen's Pirate.
3. Unfortunately, William Kidd's skirmishes at sea branded him a pirate, and he was put on trial and executed.

Day 4 (page 77)
Student answers can vary but may include:
1. During battle, Blackbeard frightened/confused his enemies by burning fuses in his beard to create a smoke effect.
2. Instead of gold, Blackbeard acquired/confiscated treasure such as barrels of sugar and cocoa.
3. Legends say that Blackbeard's body swam/circled/revolved around the ship three times after he was killed and thrown overboard.
4. Some declare/exclaim that Blackbeard was the most successful pirate, but that is simply not true.

ANSWER KEY (cont.)

Week 14: Adventures into the Unknown

Day 3 (page 81)

Student answers can vary but may include:

1. In hopes of reaching the Far East, Christopher Columbus sailed across the ocean but reached North America instead.
2. Ferdinand Magellan's crew was the first to circumnavigate the earth. Sadly, Magellan died during the journey, but his crew sailed on.
3. The adventurer, Amerigo Vespucci, discovered South America on his journey. In honor of his expedition, the Americas were named after him.

Day 4 (page 82)

Student answers can vary but may include:

1. Columbus begged/lobbied/petitioned the king of Portugal to fund an expedition.
2. The queen admired/respected/appreciated explorers, and so she gave Columbus the money and three ships to explore the uncharted waters.
3. Columbus assumed/believed/understood where he landed was near India, so he called the natives *Indians*.
4. In all, Columbus journeyed/navigated/traversed four times to the New World.

Day 5 (page 83)

See Narrative Writing Rubric on page 208.

Week 15: Building Bridges

Day 2 (page 85)

E: What amazing structures bridges are!; D: You may have noticed that bridges often look different from one another.; D: Engineers build four main types of bridges: beam bridges, truss bridges, arch bridges, and suspension bridges.; D: They have a few things to consider when deciding which type to build.; IN: What kinds of materials are available? IN: How long does the bridge need to be?; D: The answers to these questions help them decide on the shape, size, and type of bridge that they will build.; IM: The next time you cross a bridge, pause for a moment and think about what went into building it.

Day 3 (page 86)

Student answers can vary but may include:

1. Consider a few things before deciding on the type of bridge you will build.
2. I can't believe how different bridges can look from each other!
3. Have you ever thought how engineers decide on the shape, size, and type of bridge that they will build?

Day 4 (page 87)

1. Most beam bridges are less than 250 feet (76 meters) long. **A** beam bridge looks like a long, straight line. **The** beam is heavy**,** so it has to be a shorter bridge. **Otherwise**, it will collapse.
2. The bridge that can span the farthest is the suspension bridge. **A** suspension bridge is suspended in air by cables.
3. The bridge with the most strength is the arch bridge. **Arch** bridges can carry the most weight because of the design of the arch. **Long** ago**,** the Romans used these types of bridges.
4. Perhaps the most complex bridge is the truss bridge. **A** truss bridge is a bridge supported by frames of beams in a triangular shape. **These** trusses work together to hold up the bridge.

Week 16: Designing Parachutes

Day 3 (page 91)

Student answers can vary but may include:

1. Imperative sentence: Use a ribbon-ring parachute when falling at a fast speed.
   Exclamatory sentence: Ribbon-ring parachutes don't break, even when falling at a fast speed!
2. Exclamatory sentence: Amazingly, the force of the air does not break the parachute!
   Interrogative sentence: How does the force of the air not break the parachute?
3. Interrogative sentence: How many different types of parachutes are there?
   Imperative sentence. Think about all the many different types of parachutes!

Day 4 (page 92)

Student answers can vary but may include.

1. Skydivers prefer square parachutes. **The** shape reduces swinging movements.
2. Ram-air parachutes help control speed and direction. **So**, this makes them ideal for people needing to land in particular places and at controlled speeds. **The** force of the air does not break the ram-air parachute.
3. Ribbon-ring parachutes have openings that allow air to pass through. **This** keeps the parachute from breaking**,** even if it is traveling at a high speed**.**
4. Cargo can be heavy**,** so a round parachute is used because the shape offers the most drag. **This** way**,** the cargo does not drop at a high speed and can land safely.

Day 5 (page 93)

See Informative/Explanatory Writing Rubric on page 207.

ANSWER KEY *(cont.)*

Week 17: Groundhog Day

Day 1 (page 94)

Check circles:
Groundhog Day should be celebrated because most students like to learn about groundhogs and the weather during that time of year.

Groundhog Day should not be celebrated because it is not an accurate way to predict the weather.

Groundhog Day should be celebrated because it is a German tradition that has been around for hundreds of years.

Day 3 (page 96)

Example answers include:
1. Claims should not include statements like "I think."
2. This statement does not make an official claim but just gives information.
3. This is a well-written claim because it states the subject, gives the opinion about the topic, and then provides reasons for the claim.

Day 4 (page 97)

According to superstition**,** the sun caused the groundhog to see his shadow**,** and the shadow would frighten the groundhog back into hibernation. If it were cloudy**,** then the groundhog would not be frightened back into hibernation. Spring would come early. Farmers depended on this information to plant crops. However**,** the groundhog was not always accurate in predicting the weather. This caused many farmers to lose their crops**,** and many of them went broke.

Week 18: Daylight Saving Time

Day 3 (page 101)
1. Since receiving vitamin D supports the idea about daylight saving time promoting better health, the two sentences can be combined.
2. Since daylight saving time allowed for another hour of work, directly supporting the need for more workers, the sentences can be combined.
3. The second sentence provides evidence to support the first sentence, so the sentences should be combined.

Day 4 (page 102)
1. ~~I think that~~ Daylight saving time should be mandated for all states and territories because it would keep everyone on the same schedule no matter where they lived.
2. This claim is accurate.
3. ~~I feel that~~ Daylight saving time should not be used because it is not adhered to in all states, it causes confusion for travelers, and it does not add value to people's extracurricular activities.
4. This claim is accurate.

Day 5 (page 103)
See Argument Writing Rubric on page 206.

Week 19: Superhero Origins

Day 1 (page 104)

Checked circles:
Metal Man was created during the Cold War.

Metal Man was meant to be a symbol of weapons of mass destruction.

Metal Man's armor is designed for protection.

Although Metal Man has no superpowers, he does have his armor.

Day 3 (page 106)
1. Feminism and women's rights mean the same thing. Students will select one of these to use.
2. Foes and enemies mean the same thing. Students will select one of these to use.
3. Bullied and pushed around mean the same thing. Students will select one of these to use.
4. Hope and promise mean the same thing. Students will select one of these to use.

Week 20: Superhero Powers

Day 4 (page 112)
1. *Honest* and *tell the truth* mean the same thing.
2. *Responds* and *reacts* mean the same thing.
3. *Skill* and *ability* mean the same thing.

Day 5 (page 113)
See Informative/Explanatory Writing Rubric on page 207.

ANSWER KEY (cont.)

Week 21: Black Holes

Day 1 (page 114)

A black hole can be as small as an atom.

A tiny black hole has the mass of a mountain.

A very large black hole can have mass that is 20 times larger than the mass found in the sun.

A supermassive black hole is larger than the mass of 1 million suns.

Gravity pulls light into the middles of black holes, so scientists cannot see black holes.

Day 2 (page 115)

<u>Black holes</u> are not empty spaces. Within a black hole, <u>gravity</u> is so strong that everything is pulled inside. For example, a black hole's <u>gravity</u> can squeeze a star that is 10 times more massive than the sun into a space that is the size of a modern day city. A tiny black hole has the <u>mass</u> of a mountain even though it is as small as an atom. A very large black hole can have <u>mass</u> that is 20 times larger than the <u>mass</u> found in the sun. A <u>supermassive black hole</u> is larger than the mass of 1 million suns.

Day 4 (page 117)

1. A black hole, as large as it seems, can be as small as an atom.
2. A tiny black hole has the mass of a mountain, a concept that seems amazing to many people.
3. A very large black hole, a fact that can be inconceivable for most people, can have mass that is 20 times larger than the mass found in the sun.
4. A supermassive black hole, something only usually shown in movies, is larger than the mass of 1 million suns.
5. Gravity pulls light into the middles of black holes, so scientists cannot see black holes.

Week 22: Space Travel

Day 1 (page 119)

Example answers include:

Yes, because it is talking about future space.

No, because it states an opinion.

No, because it states an opinion.

Yes, because it provides facts about space travel.

No because it's talking about fictional movies.

Day 4 (page 122)

1. NASA is planning on taking humans to the moon again by the year 2020 in preparation for travel to Mars, something only the adventurous would do.
2. Humans, the brave ones anyway, dream of traveling to Mars but know they will be unable to return back to Earth.
3. Some people think space travel, that is travel outside of our atmosphere, is the most exciting type of travel.
4. NASA plans on using the *Orion* capsule, a new type of spaceship, for human travel because it is safer than the shuttle used in past years.
5. In the movies, people travel from planet to planet in a matter of hours, which is something completely fictional.

Day 5 (page 123)

See Informative/Explanatory Writing Rubric on page 207.

Week 23: Live Theater Scripts

Day 3 (page 126)

Students may cross out *queasy* or *nauseated*.

Students may cross out *lady's maid* or *servant*.

Students may cross out *hurry* or *act quickly*.

Students may cross out *momentarily* or *shortly*.

Day 4 (page 127)

1. The **classic** story of **Cinderella** is one that most people know.
2. One undeveloped character that we know very little about is **Prince** Charming.
3. The **wicked stepmother** is a common character found in scripts.
4. Even with **Cinderella** being the main character, the **audience** really knows little about her.
5. **Fairy Godmother** saves the day by giving Cinderella a dress and a way to the ball.

ANSWER KEY *(cont.)*

Week 24: Television Show Scripts

Day 3 (page 131)

1. Since *angry* is a synonym of *mad*, it does not make sense to have both words in the sentence.
2. Since *worker* is a synonym of *laborer*, it does not make sense to have both words in the sentence.
3. Since *weak* is a synonym of *frail*, it does not make sense to have both words in the sentence.
4. Since *job* is a synonym of *profession*, it does not make sense to have both words in the sentence.

Day 4 (page 132)

1. Many shows on **television** are **comedies**, which are designed to make people laugh.
2. Television **scripts** are similar to theater scripts in that they both tell the characters what to say.
3. It is important that **scripts** tell the storyline in words and actions.
4. **Writers** of **scripts** should strive to use the strongest words that describe something.
5. Cartoons are **television shows** that can be designed for both children and adults depending on the content.

Day 5 (page 133)

See Narrative Writing Rubric on page 208.

Week 25: Comic Strips

Day 3 (page 136)

1. metaphor: <u>Writing reports</u> is <u>rain on a cloudy day</u>.
2. alliteration: <u>Radical reports read ridiculously</u>, so read them carefully.
3. hyperbole and simile: I once saw a <u>desk that was as big as a house!</u>
4. onomatopoeia: <u>Thump!</u> The boss threw a stack of reports on the worker's desk.
5. simile: Being a <u>boss</u> is like being a <u>king</u>.

Day 4 (page 137)

1. Comic strips and movie reviews are often opinion pieces found in newspapers.
2. Comic strips can contain both animals and people.
3. Writers often find it easier to express opinions and thoughts using comic strips because they poke fun at ideas and things.
4. Since most comic strips are made up of dialogue, it is not necessary to use quotation marks and commas.
5. Animals such as cats and dogs, often take on human characteristics in comic strips.

Week 26: Movie Reviews

Day 1 (page 139)

Students' reasons may vary.

1. F
2. T
3. T
4. F
5. T

Day 3 (page 141)

1. metaphor: <u>Movies</u> are <u>time outs</u> in a busy world.
2. alliteration: <u>Movies mostly make me mad</u>, but only because I know they are not true stories.
3. hyperbole and simile: I once saw a <u>movie that was as long as a year!</u>
4. onomatopoeia: <u>Crash!</u> The pot landed on the floor and the actor jumped to his feet.
5. simile: <u>Seeing movies</u> is <u>like living dreams</u> through other people.

Day 4 (page 142)

1. Movie reviews have both summaries and opinions of the movie being reviewed.
2. People often consult movie reviews, either online or in print, when deciding to see a movie.
3. Responsible movie reviewers always give reasons for their opinions and ideas they express in these reviews.
4. A helpful tip for writers is to use figurative language to make the movie reviews more interesting to readers and audiences.
5. Movie reviews are somewhat similar to comic strips in that they both express opinions and are found in newspapers.

Day 5 (page 143)

See Argument Writing Rubric on page 206.

ANSWER KEY *(cont.)*

Week 27: Fantasy Creatures

Day 1 (page 144)

can tell made-up stories about creatures, can have creatures that go on quests, can include real or imagined creatures, can include novels about creatures, can be short stories about creatures, can include picture books about creatures, can have beginnings, middles, and ends to stories that include creatures, can have settings where creatures interact with one another

Day 4 (page 147)

1. If the dragon really wanted to stop the wizard and his elves, <u>he/she</u> can burn the forest down with one breath of fire.
2. Most people believe that dragons are fierce, but what would happen in a story if <u>they</u> were afraid of fire?
3. When one goes on a serious quest, <u>he/she</u> has to be ready for hardship and encounters with terrible creatures.
4. The elves ran out of bows and had to revert to karate to protect <u>their</u> wizard.
5. When the wizard finally found the magic lamp, <u>he</u> had to be careful not to wake the sleeping bats guarding it.

Week 28: Fantasy Quests

Day 1 (page 149)

The Purposeless Magic: Good title for a fantasy because it lends itself to a story, not informational text.

The Source of the Mask: Good title for a fantasy because it lends itself to a story, not informational text.

How to Write Best Selling Fantasy Novels: Not a good title for a fantasy because it lends itself to a how-to informational text.

Getting Your Fantasy Novel Published: Not a good title for a fantasy because it lends itself to a how-to informational text.

The Family Thorn: Good title for a fantasy because it lends itself to a story, not informational text.

Gift in the Castle: Good title for a fantasy because it lends itself to a story, not informational text.

Ember in the Glass: Good title for a fantasy because it lends itself to a story, not informational text.

Day 4 (page 152)

The dragon was exhausted as <u>he</u> looked back at the burning forest. He had no breath left and therefore no fire or smoke when <u>he</u> suddenly saw the wizard and his entourage hiding behind the last tree standing. How did <u>they</u> escape my fury? he questioned. Then, <u>they</u> ran for the mountain expecting to be burned in the process, but the dragon had nothing left to threaten them with except <u>his</u> large body.

Day 5 (page 153)

See Narrative Writing Rubric on page 208.

Week 29: Rights and Equality

Day 1 (page 154)

Gaining the right to vote was a step forward in equal rights for women.

Today, many believe that people should get equal pay for equal work, regardless if they are male or female.

The fight for equal rights is something that is still ongoing today.

Because of the Civil Rights movement, schools became desegregated and African Americans learned alongside white children.

Day 3 (page 156)

1. Claims should not include statements like "I think."
2. It just gives information not make an official claim.
3. Claims should not include statements like "I think."

Day 4 (page 157)

Some people think that equal rights were settled long ago**, but** people around the world are still fighting for equal rights. First, when families have to pay for an education, they send their sons**, and** the daughters stay home to help their mothers run the family. Girls that do attend school to learn to write, read, and count may eventually have children of their own**, and** they will educate this family, too.

ANSWER KEY *(cont.)*

Week 30: Diversity

Day 3 (page 161)

1. The claim uses the terms "I think," and a strong claim omits those words.
2. This claim is not supported by evidence.
3. The claim uses the terms "I feel," and a strong claim omits those words.

Day 4 (page 162)

1. People form opinions based on their backgrounds and experiences, **because** what happened to them at some point in their lives affects how they view the world.
2. Other workers who are doing the same job are being paid more money because of their skin colors, **so** this experience will most likely affect how this person feels about the topic of equal pay.
3. This experience will most likely affect how this person feels about the topic of equal pay, **and** other people, who have never had this experience, can learn from this person's experience.

Day 5 (page 163)

See Argument Writing Rubric on page 206.

Week 31: Lacrosse

Day 1 (page 164)

American Indians, the first to play lacrosse, played to settle disputes, for spiritual reasons, to heal illnesses, and as a preparation for war.; To play the game, players use lacrosse sticks and other protective gear, such as goggles and helmets.; About 300 years ago, the Iroquois first introduced lacrosse to Europeans.; There are different rules for men's and women's lacrosse, with men's lacrosse being more physical.; The object of the game is to advance the ball into the goal guarded by the goalie.

Day 4 (page 167)

1. The game of lacrosse, the fastest growing sport in the United States, is played with sticks and a ball.
2. Players advance the ball, which is small and hard, down the field by throwing it and running with it.
3. American Indians, the first to play lacrosse, played to settle disputes, for spiritual reasons, to heal illnesses, and as a preparation for war.
4. There are different rules for men and women's lacrosse, with men's lacrosse using more contact.
5. The object of the game is to advance the ball into the goal, which is guarded by the goalie.

Week 32: Rugby

Day 4 (page 172)

1. The game of rugby, one of the most aggressive sports today, is played on a field that is 100 meters long.
2. Players advance the ball down the field by both kicking it and running with it, but not throwing it forward.
3. A try, one way to score a point, is when a player takes the ball to the goal and places it on the ground with a hand on top of the ball.
4. A goal, another way to score a point, is when the player kicks the ball inside the goal and above the crossbar.
5. The object of the game, which is a difficult one to do, is to score more points than your opponent within an 80-minute time frame.

Day 5 (page 173)

See Informative/Explanatory Writing Rubric on page 207.

ANSWER KEY *(cont.)*

Week 33: Domestic Pets

Day 1 (page 174)

Some families are unable to have certain pets because of allergies.; To raise a dog, a family must be willing to feed and take care of the dog's needs.; Pets, such as cats, need attention, love, food, and shelter.; For some, fish make the ultimate pet because they are less demanding.; Some people adopt pets from shelters or rescue groups, while others get their pets from breeders.

Day 2 (page 175)

(IN)Have you ever thought of the benefits of owning a pet? (D) Studies show that pets can improve the health and well being of people. (D)For example, research shows that children who live in homes with cats and dogs have fewer chances of developing allergies. (D)They also have higher immune systems as they grow older. (D)Pets have shown to reduce blood pressure in older adults. (E)Pets can even reduce anxiety! (IM)So, before you take medicine for a health problem, think about getting a pet first.

Day 3 (page 176)

1. About 62 percent of families, two out of every three, in the United States own pets.
2. Some people, such as older generations who live alone, own pets because they want companionship.
3. While some people get their pets from breeders and stores, others go to shelters, places where people can adopt pets, to find the newest members of their households.
4. Owning pets, something that two out of three families do, has been proven to offer health benefits like lowered blood pressure.

Day 4 (page 177)

1. Many people enjoy pets, because pets do not judge them based on appearance or social status.
2. Pets do not care whether people are beautiful or ugly; they simply are loyal to their owners.
3. Since fish can have a calming effect on people, many doctors have large fish and small fish in their waiting rooms. (no corrections)
4. Because pets do depend on their owners for food and shelter, many parents use pets as a way of teaching their children responsibility.
5. Animals, such as dogs and horses, can help their owners get more exercise, because most dogs require walks every day.

Week 34: Exotic Pets

Day 3 (page 181)

1. Even though tarantulas have venomous bites, something comparable to a wasp sting, many people still choose to own them as pets. (nonrestrictive)
2. The bearded dragon, which is very social and likes to hang out on its owner's shoulders, can live anywhere from 10 to 20 years. (nonrestrictive)
3. The flying squirrel, originally a nocturnal animal, can adapt to being awake during the day to socialize with its owners. (restrictive)

Day 4 (page 182)

1. A flying squirrel uses a gliding membrane to fly in a downward direction and needs room to run and jump.
2. Bearded dragons need environments with just the right temperatures and UV lights.
3. For someone wanting a pet to live a long time, tarantulas can be the ideal pet because they can live up to 20 years.
4. Owners of tarantulas should avoid touching it too often, because too much handling can cause the tarantula to be stressed.
5. Exotic pets are not for everyone, but they can make great pets for some people who are willing to make accommodations.

Day 5 (page 183)

See Informative/Explanatory Writing Rubric on page 207.

ANSWER KEY *(cont.)*

Week 35: Eating

Day 1 (page 184)

1. This sentence doesn't make a good case for an argument paragraph because it uses the words "I think."
2. This sentence makes a good case for an argument paragraph because it uses facts as the basis.
3. This sentence doesn't make a good case for an argument paragraph because it uses the words "I feel."
4. This sentence makes a good case for an argument paragraph because it uses facts as the basis.

Day 3 (page 186)

1. Not a strong claim because it uses the words "I think."
2. Not a strong claim because it only states vague ideas.
3. This is a strong claim.
4. Not a strong claim because it uses the words "I feel."

Day 4 (page 187)

Some people might doubt the importance of eating healthy, **but** the latest research seems to prove that good nutrients affect our brains, movement, and bodies.

Every now and then, it might be okay to enjoy a cupcake, **but** it's best to stick to a nutritious diet if we want our brains and bodies to stay healthy.

Week 36: Exercising

Day 3 (page 191)

1. Studies show that students who exercise are better problem solvers, **so** if you want to think more creatively, you need to exercise.
2. Exercising helps students develop stronger bones, **so** students should strive to get more exercise every day.
3. Doctors worry about student's health, **because** more and more students spend time inside playing video games instead of playing sports outdoors.

Day 4 (page 192)

1. I think that exercise helps students, because studies show it promotes better sleeping at night and thinking during the day.
2. Exercise is important because it builds students' problem-solving skills and creative thinking skills.
3. I feel that exercise is important because it promotes better bone and muscle growth in students.
4. Students should strive to get more exercise, because studies show there are great benefits to their bodies, minds, and habits.

Day 5 (page 193)

See Argument Writing Rubric on page 206.

ARGUMENT WRITING RUBRIC

Directions: Evaluate students' work in each category by circling one number in each row. Students have opportunities to score up to five points in each row and up to 15 points total.

	Exceptional Writing	**Quality Writing**	**Developing Writing**
Focus and Organization	Clearly states an argument that is relevant to the topic. Demonstrates clear understanding of the intended audience and purpose of the piece. Organizes ideas in a purposeful way and includes an introduction, a detailed body, and a conclusion.	States an argument that is relevant to the topic. Demonstrates some understanding of the intended audience and purpose of the piece. Organizes ideas and includes an introduction, a body, and a conclusion.	States an unclear argument that is not fully relevant to the topic. Demonstrates little understanding of the intended audience or purpose of the piece. Does not include an introduction, a body, or a conclusion.
Points	5 4	3 2	1 0
Written Expression	Uses descriptive and precise language with clarity and intention. Maintains a consistent voice and uses an appropriate tone that supports meaning. Uses multiple sentence types and transitions smoothly between ideas.	Uses a broad vocabulary. Maintains a consistent voice and supports a tone and feeling through language. Varies sentence length and word choices.	Uses a limited or an unvaried vocabulary. Provides an inconsistent or a weak voice and tone. Provides little to no variation in sentence type and length.
Points	5 4	3 2	1 0
Language Conventions	Capitalizes, punctuates, and spells accurately. Demonstrates complete thoughts within sentences, with accurate subject-verb agreement. Uses paragraphs appropriately and with clear purpose.	Capitalizes, punctuates, and spells accurately. Demonstrates complete thoughts within sentences and appropriate grammar. Paragraphs are properly divided and supported.	Incorrectly capitalizes, punctuates, and spells. Uses fragmented or run-on sentences. Utilizes poor grammar overall. Paragraphs are poorly divided and developed.
Points	5 4	3 2	1 0

Total Points: _____

INFORMATIVE/EXPLANATORY WRITING RUBRIC

Directions: Evaluate students' work in each category by circling one number in each row. Students have opportunities to score up to five points in each row and up to 15 points total.

	Exceptional Writing	Quality Writing	Developing Writing
Focus and Organization	Clearly states the topic and purposefully develops it throughout the writing. Demonstrates clear understanding of the intended audience and purpose of the piece. Organizes the information into a well-supported introduction, body, and conclusion.	States the topic and develops it throughout the writing. Demonstrates some understanding of the intended audience and purpose of the piece. Organizes the information into an introduction, body, and conclusion.	Does not state the topic and/or develop it throughout the writing. Demonstrates little understanding of the intended audience or purpose of the piece. Fails to organize the information into an introduction, body, or conclusion.
Points	5 4	3 2	1 0
Written Expression	Uses descriptive and precise language with clarity and intention. Maintains a consistent voice and uses an appropriate tone that supports meaning. Uses multiple sentence types and transitions smoothly between ideas.	Uses a broad vocabulary. Maintains a consistent voice and supports a tone and feeling through language. Varies sentence length and word choices.	Uses a limited or an unvaried vocabulary. Provides an inconsistent or a weak voice and tone. Provides little to no variation in sentence type and length.
Points	5 4	3 2	1 0
Language Conventions	Capitalizes, punctuates, and spells accurately. Demonstrates complete thoughts within sentences, with accurate subject-verb agreement. Uses paragraphs appropriately and with clear purpose.	Capitalizes, punctuates, and spells accurately. Demonstrates complete thoughts within sentences and appropriate grammar. Paragraphs are properly divided and supported.	Incorrectly capitalizes, punctuates, and spells. Uses fragmented or run-on sentences. Utilizes poor grammar overall. Paragraphs are poorly divided and developed.
Points	5 4	3 2	1 0

Total Points: _____

NARRATIVE WRITING RUBRIC

Directions: Evaluate students' work in each category by circling one number in each row. Students have opportunities to score up to five points in each row and up to 15 points total.

	Exceptional Writing	Quality Writing	Developing Writing
Focus and Organization	Identifies the topic of the story and maintains the focus throughout the writing. Develops clear settings, a strong plot, and interesting characters. Demonstrates clear understanding of the intended audience and purpose of the piece. Engages the reader from the opening hook through the middle to the conclusion.	Identifies the topic of the story, but has some trouble maintaining the focus throughout the writing. Develops settings, a plot, and characters. Demonstrates some understanding of the intended audience and purpose of the piece. Includes an interesting opening, a strong story, and a conclusion.	Fails to identify the topic of the story or maintain focus throughout the writing. Does not develop strong settings, plot, or characters. Demonstrates little understanding of the intended audience or purpose of the piece. Provides lack of clarity in the beginning, middle, and/or conclusion.
Points	5 4	3 2	1 0
Written Expression	Uses descriptive and precise language with clarity and intention. Maintains a consistent voice and uses an appropriate tone that supports meaning. Uses multiple sentence types and transitions smoothly between ideas.	Uses a broad vocabulary. Maintains a consistent voice and supports a tone and feeling through language. Varies sentence length and word choices.	Uses a limited or an unvaried vocabulary. Provides an inconsistent or a weak voice and tone. Provides little to no variation in sentence type and length.
Points	5 4	3 2	1 0
Language Conventions	Capitalizes, punctuates, and spells accurately. Demonstrates complete thoughts within sentences, with accurate subject-verb agreement. Uses paragraphs appropriately and with clear purpose.	Capitalizes, punctuates, and spells accurately. Demonstrates complete thoughts within sentences and appropriate grammar. Paragraphs are properly divided and supported.	Incorrectly capitalizes, punctuates, and spells. Uses fragmented or run-on sentences. Utilizes poor grammar overall. Paragraphs are poorly divided and developed.
Points	5 4	3 2	1 0

Total Points: _____

#51529—180 Days of Writing   © *Shell Education*

ARGUMENT WRITING ANALYSIS

Directions: Record each student's rubric scores (page 206) in the appropriate columns. Add the totals every two weeks and record the sums in the Total Scores column. You can view: (1) which students are not understanding the opinion genre and (2) how students progress after multiple encounters with the opinion genre.

Student Name	Week 6	Week 8	Week 18	Week 26	Week 30	Week 36	Total Scores
Average Classroom Score							

INFORMATIVE/EXPLANATORY WRITING ANALYSIS

Directions: Record each student's rubric score (page 207) in the appropriate columns. Add the totals every two weeks and record the sums in the Total Scores column. You can view: (1) which students are not understanding the informative/explanatory genre and (2) how students progress after multiple encounters with the informative/explanatory genre.

Student Name	Week 4	Week 16	Week 20	Week 22	Week 32	Week 34	Total Scores
Average Classroom Score							

NARRATIVE WRITING ANALYSIS

Directions: Record each student's rubric score (page 208) in the appropriate columns. Add the totals every two weeks and record the sums in the Total Scores column. You can view: (1) which students are not understanding the narrative genre and (2) how students progress after multiple encounters with the narrative genre.

Student Name	Week 2	Week 10	Week 12	Week 14	Week 24	Week 28	Total Scores
Average Classroom Score							

THE WRITING PROCESS

STEP 1: PREWRITING

Think about the topic. Brainstorm ideas, and plan what you want to include in your writing.

STEP 2: DRAFTING

Use your brainstormed ideas to write a first draft. Don't worry about errors. This will be a rough draft.

STEP 3: REVISING

Read your rough draft. Think about the vocabulary you used and how your writing is organized. Then, make the appropriate changes to improve your written piece.

STEP 4: EDITING

Reread your revised draft. Check for errors in spelling, punctuation, and grammar. Use editing marks to correct the errors.

STEP 5: PUBLISHING

Create a final version of your piece, including the corrections from the edited version. Be sure to reread your work for any errors.

EDITING MARKS

Editing Marks	Symbol Names	Example
≡	capitalization symbol	david gobbled up the grapes.
/	lowercase symbol	My mother hugged Me when I Came Home.
⊙	insert period symbol	The clouds danced in the sky.
sp ◯	check spelling symbol	I laffed at the story.
∿	transpose symbol	How you are?
∧	insert symbol	Would you please pass the pizza?
⌄,	insert comma symbol	I have two cats, two dogs and a goldfish.
" " ∨ ∨	insert quotations symbol	That's amazing, she shouted.
℘	deletion symbol	Will you call call me on the phone tonight?
¶	new paragraph symbol	... in the tree. ¶After lunch, I spent the day...
#	add space symbol	I ran tothe tree.

ARGUMENT WRITING TIPS

Ask yourself . . .	Remember . . .
Do I have a strong belief in my claim so that I can convince others to believe the same?	Make sure you can back up your claim with specific examples.
Have I stated my opinion in a way that grabs the reader's attention?	Begin with a question or a bold statement that includes your claim.
Do I have at least three reasons based on facts for my claim?	Include at least three solid reasons why the reader should agree with you.
Do I have an example for each reason that strengthens my argument?	Each reason must be followed by one strong example.
Do I have a logical order to my writing?	Don't bounce around. Focus on a logical order to present each reason and example.
Am I using smooth transitions to connect my thoughts and help my writing flow?	Use transition words like *first*, *in addition to*, *another reason*, and *most important*.
Does my conclusion restate my claim?	Do not forget to restate your claim in the final sentence.
Have I used correct spelling, grammar, and punctuation?	Revisit what you have written. Then, check for mistakes.

INFORMATIVE/EXPLANATORY WRITING TIPS

Ask yourself . . .

Remember . . .

Ask yourself . . .	Remember . . .
Do I provide enough information on the topic?	Make sure to include facts about the topic in your writing so that the reader is informed.
Have I narrowed the focus of the topic?	Choose one aspect of the topic that you want to write about.
Does my writing have a hook?	Begin with a strong topic sentence that grabs the reader's attention.
Is my information presented in a logical order?	Do not bounce around. Present each topic sentence at the beginning of a paragraph and add details.
Have I included enough information that the reader will be interested in learning even more?	End with a strong sentence that makes the reader want to learn more about the subject.
Have I used correct spelling, grammar, and punctuation?	Revisit what you have written. Then, check for mistakes.

NARRATIVE WRITING TIPS

Ask yourself . . .

	Remember . . .

Ask yourself . . .

Am I the main character? Is the story told from my point of view?

Remember . . .

You are in the story, telling where you are, what you see, who you are with, and what you do.

Does my story have a hook?

Include an exciting introductory sentence that makes the reader want to continue reading.

Does my story make sense and have a beginning, a middle, and an end?

Do not bounce around. Focus on a logical order of how the experience happened.

Am I using transitions to connect my thoughts and help the writing flow?

Use transition words like *first*, *next*, *then*, *another*, and *finally*.

Am I including rich details and sensory language to help paint a picture in the reader's mind?

Use lots of adjectives, and incorporate figurative language, such as metaphors and similes, to make your story come to life.

Does my conclusion summarize the main idea?

Incorporate a sentence or two that reflects on what you have written.

Have I used correct spelling, grammar, and punctuation?

Revisit what you have written. Then, check for mistakes.

Argument Writing

Informative/Explanatory Writing

Narrative Writing

PEER/SELF-EDITING CHECKLIST

Directions: Place a check mark in front of each item as you check it.

❏ The writing clearly states an argument. (argument writing only)

❏ The writing clearly states the topic. (informative/explanatory writing only)

❏ The writing has an engaging beginning.

❏ The writing includes details to support the opinion/topic.

❏ The writing has a strong conclusion.

❏ The writing follows a logical order.

❏ Lots of interesting words are used.

❏ Words are capitalized correctly.

❏ Words are spelled correctly.

❏ There is correct punctuation.

CONTENTS OF THE DIGITAL RESOURCE CD

Teacher Resources

Resource	Filename
Writing Rubrics	writingrubrics.pdf
Argument Writing Analysis	argumentpageitem.pdf argumentpageitem.doc argumentpageitem.xls
Informative/Explanatory Writing Analysis	informativepageitem.pdf informativepageitem.doc informativepageitem.xls
Narrative Writing Analysis	narrativepageitem.pdf narrativepageitem.doc narrativepageitem.xls
Writing Signs	writingsigns.pdf
Standards Charts	standards.pdf

Student Resources

All of the 180 practice pages are contained in a single PDF. To print specific days, open the PDF and select the pages to print.

Resource	Filename
Practice Pages	practicepages.pdf
Writing Tips	writingtips.pdf
Writing Prompts	writingprompts.pdf
The Writing Process	writingprocess.pdf
Editing Marks	editingmarks.pdf
Peer/Self-Editing Checklist	editingchecklist.pdf

NOTES

NOTES

NOTES

9 781425 815295